I0142340

DEDICATED: to the usual suspects.....my extended family, and to the many researchers who believe the past must be uncovered, to impact the present, to alter the future.

"...It is human nature to take up causes whereby a man may oppress his neighbor no matter how unjustly, hence they have no trouble finding men who would preach the damnability and heresy of the new doctrine from their very pulpit..."   Galileo Galilei
(Convicted of heresy by the Church, threatened with torture ,placed on house arrest until he died).

The former Pope, Benedict XVI, was the worlds modern day Inquisitor for many years before his election to Pope. His title was the Prefect for the Doctrine Of The Congregation Of Faith.

PROLOGUE

In this sequel of Chronicles of Jongleur, the Storyteller, the inquisition of the 13th century is still going strong in 1254 A.D., ten years after the earlier story ends. Father Simon has left his life and his religion in Britain after coming to grips from a trauma of terrible news. News of the last member of a family he knew, and watched from afar for years.

Before he left, he set far to the chronicle which held that news. Along with it he burned his cabin home, the chapel of the country monastery where he taught Latin to young men who would be priests.

For these ten years the old man has been walking the mountains and valleys of France in search of someone he may never find. In this saga you will see what drives the man, Simon, for he calls himself only a monk, now.

You will follow a man on the mission of a lifetime. You will also see the Inquisition ,up close and personal, just as thousands of innocent people belonging to various rebel religious sects did at the time; tracked down and forced to wear the signs of outcasts losing their property, that is ,if they were even allowed to live. They

left their homes and property, fleeing to the mountains all over
Europe, especially in France. And some walked into the prepared
bonfires instead , exhausted from running, unwilling to give up their
way of worship, one that legends say was brought from the holy land
a thousand years before.

      You will be handed a slice of truth to taste, a tidbit of history
to contemplate. You will have an opportunity to see what daily fear
was like for the people in Europe, and this saga ,just as in many
eastern parts of the world today.

      You will, no doubt, take note that nothing has changed in the
world's religions in two thousand years, even as you read this. It is a
tale with some truths , some history - some earthly devils , and some
earthly angels. You will be a witness to history. I have taken
liberties by using fictional names and events to illustrate the real
stories that have come down through the ages, that were not
destroyed. This is your challenge, to decide what was history . Most
of the records were eliminated to hide the shame of this history.
What little is left tells a great deal of what happened.

CHAPTER 1

1254 A.D.,Bugarag mountain, Southern France

Halfway up the mountain the old priest put his foot down just
wrong enough for it to slip on the lose gravel, and turn his sandal
sideway. His ankle snapped. The pain was acute, and his reflexes were
too slow to stop the fall down the steep cliff that separated solid
ground from solid limestone . That very spot would have shown him
that the cliff , where he fell, loomed upward to the summit , the top of
the four thousand foot mountain.

He was blessedly unconscious by the time he stopped rolling,
for the plateau had stopped his fall, a steep hillside halfway up the
mountain. Unconscious in a thicket filled with low trees and scrub, he
was hidden from any eyes who might have helped him, if there had
been any eyes that far up the mountain.

The grove of trees saved his life from the unforgiving elements
of sun, wind and water, but the body that fell had the soft constitution
of a man whose life work had been done with his mind until the last
few years. Now the mountain hid him from anyone who might

find him on its wild terrain. He would think, later, that only God was there to save him in that high place. But later , thinking would be too difficult for his pain-racked old flesh and bones. He would remember through the pain his last thought had been that this high chapperel was a wasteland. He would wonder if, once again, the climb he was making was a waste of time for whom he was seeking here.

Chapter 2

1254 A.D. , Toulouse, France, The Villa

There have always been twelve of us. If you are reading these words then you know nothing of us for I am, no doubt, the first and only to tell of us. That is only if the Order has allowed this to survive and be found. If so I must start from the beginning, for you must be somewhere in the future,and I pen this for the future to know.

We twelve are the sentinels of this time, but in time before us twelve others have watched, and recorded , history of the known world for the Order. If you have found this writing in some library, some ruin in time, and have come seeking the truth then you must leave your history books behind you, for history serves its own master, and recognizes only its master's voice.

Why do I write this, you may ask? What could be so important that I would take a chance of discovery and the penalties that it would bring? Why would I risk my reputation with the Order and the chance they will not let my efforts see the future by exposing them? It will be made known for the future to answer that.

In the Order we are always twelve, as I have mentioned, and will always be twelve. Each of the sentinels is appointed for life- but long before our life has ended our replacement has been selected and trained. We have existed only as long as the written word, though in our archives there is some evidence that some peoples in the past used the spoken word long before ,to carry some message to the next generation.

They would have been the first keepers of the truth, the first sentinels. Those who chose to disagree with what they said merely called their messages legends. I suppose that may be why man learned to make a scrawl, in order to express himself in some way, in order to pass his truths along. And when that happened those who had a different motive scrawled another version.

The Order guards the reality of how mankind has lived, and record it for the ages. It has no other agenda in time other than that truth shall not be distorted by man from any age, and I am sure the task has been more than difficult.

The guideline for the twelve has never changed. Each sentinel is been selected from a young age on the basis of character and the ability for discretion, as well as other learned skills. Each of us has been hand selected by some unknown panel within the Order. Chosen and groomed for a lifetime of service without the ordinary difficulties that other people have for survival. No sentinel ever has to worry about food, lodging, or the comfort of the families left behind. Above all, we must be above average in literacy and languages, must commit to a lifetime of service, and forgo any personal desire for marriage, position or family. As it happens not many of us have families. That should be no surprise given the wars, diseases, and other dangers of this time. I write from the thirteenth century, a time where there is no trust from neighbor to neighbor, servant to master, church to church, politician to politician, even father to child.

Our work, our constant duty is shrouded in secrecy while each of us also have a public life. We live over all the known world so there is a constant flow of factual information in our archives, which stretches back for centuries, if I did not say it before.

There are two sentinels in England, two in Spain, one in the low countries, one in Byzantium, two of us in France, three in Italy, and one in Jerusalem. None of the twelve knows the whereabouts of any other sentinel. I, alone, am the exception, for I am the archivist. I also record the information sent by the other eleven sentinels.

I am the one who files each report, and compiles a full monthly report to the order from them, as well as my own in this area. It is my job to filter the most important messages and information. I then file each man's report in the archive so men may refer to that time, that place, and know the reality of it. It is simple to realize the aim of the Order is that this information is for future man to know our mistakes, to learn from them, just as each generation has had the opportunity to. But wars have not ended, man has not learned.

Whats more, Holy wars have been in Europe for a hundred years, as well as in the East. You will soon see how we continue to kill our own people.

I imagine you wonder how such a secret order can exist given the frailties of mankind. Its history must be fine tuned, no thanks to me, since the Order has existed for many centuries. I will give the reader the gist of it as I have known it. Of course you may have already learned it in whatever time you are in, but I doubt it. Its secrets are remain secure.

You will understand why I think this after I have recorded what I have to say, that is if the order will allow my information to remain hidden in the archive for man to find in the future. And they know I am recording it, for I would never secrete anything from them. Not from fear, you understand. Each of us have lived in a lifetime of fear of discovery. But then the Order protects us, provides for us, respects our work, and we in turn respect the Order for who they are. If they think man is ready to know the truth they will allow this to see the light of the future. And if you are reading this, they have.

Each month twelve horsemen come to me from a network of riders provided by the Order. The network of riders brings me the report of each sentinel in his location. These are night riders but no one is the wiser as my official job is as notary to many important men, including clergymen. Men of government, high men of power, who have there own secrets and messages to deliver with their private stamp. As I reside in a villa at the edge of town there is generally no disturbance, and few locals, to see the comings and goings of messengers, and that is the way my officers of the Church, and government like it, for many times their documents are about each other. That should not be a surprising fact of any time. Of course they have their own notaries, but other business occurs that is to remain private , not for religious eyes, and not for mine. But they still must be sent, and a record kept for the sender. That is where I come in.

I have been here longer than most of the important people who have come to Toulouse so I am not in question as mine is an old and respectable position. It is a busy city anyway, filled with messengers all hours of the day as the business of the Church never ends. My messengers are always different so that no one knows them. They do not tarry. here. In that, they are like those who bring letters from village to village.

That is part of the secrecy of the Order. The messengers never know what they deliver and are well paid for their silence. I think they must be recruited at a young age. Perhaps they even have riding schools to train the many messengers who must travel far in a night, and relay with another rider when they stop. If they ever were apprehended there would be nothing they could tell except that they were sent from a central message service that serves many politicians and Churches alike.

The messages are always sealed and stamped with a coded image for each sentinel. I, in turn, read the reports and file them in an underground archive, an ancient archive in stone. It has been underground here for many lifetimes.

from century to century and is rented out. The villa is my office as well as my home.I have done business with many important men here,a notary always has a job.

When I have read the reports it is my duty to write a master copy and sent it to the Order each month. They have their own messengers and I have never known or asked where they are taken. These messengers are always dressed finer and look to be gentlemen. I would never doubt them as they always use a code word or hand sign to greet me. They always bring my small stipend each month as well, which I put away

All my other expenses are paid by the Order in yearly sums. This way there is no suspicion of how I live. I collect my notary fees by day and that is how the town thinks I survive as well as I do. Little do they know that my real work begins at night when I read, file, and add to my master report down in the archive hidden in stone. This is where centuries of scrolls and letters are packed away according to the year. A well hidden door in the villa leads to the stone stairway down, and torches that are lit each night. I have one servant who does this; and is provided by the order. He has been with me, almost from the beginning as cook and assistant in my day office , the ground floor of my villa.

Each sentinel has a position which would not arouse suspicion whether it be baker, teacher, undertaker. cook, even tax collector. The arms of the Order are very long indeed, perhaps even longer than the Church's reach.

The sentinels have only one requirement aside from reporting each month, and that is we are not to intercede no matter what the situation we see and report. It is not our duty to interfere with history,we are merely to observe and report the truth as it happens. We are to be a witness to history.

In our time, you will see, this is much more demanding than the work we do, for there are many wrongs in this part of the world especially, for it is in the name of God. Rather than write it all again using up so many nibs and quills, allow me to include the reports of the sentinel in France. This dirty business is everywhere , affecting everyone, but the one you read about here is a very special case indeed. I suppose you could call it the culmination of centuries to remove one dangerous family ,person by person, from the Earth, but thousands been removed with this family in time, especially the last one hundred years. How do I know? The archives.

1254 A.D. Corbieres Mountains, South France

CHAPTER 3

The old man awakened two days later to the touch of a
hand. The first sensation that occurred to him was intense pain. The
second was staring at the grove of trees that had no doubt saved him
from the elements while he was unconscious. Finally he noticed the
face that belonged to the hand that rested on his shoulder. A young
woman leaned over him, her red gold hair so long it touched his arm.
"Oh!", he squeezed out of cracked and swollen lips, "Is this Heaven?
Am I in Heaven now?"

He looked at the angel above him and tried to touch her but it
was too painful to reach, "Shhhh" she said, "Shhhh, she took his cold
hands and massaged them before laying them back on his chest, and
checked his other injuries . "Are you an angel?" he tried to say but
the words stuck to the roof of his mouth in garbled words.

He began to whimper now with the searing pain running up
and down his body. He couldn't seem to move but he could not take
his eyes off her either. She had to be an angel if he was dead. But he
couldn't be dead, not with this pain. She held a hide of water to his
lips but he could not drink. She poured a few drops on his lips. It
stung so he must be alive! Alive with pain.

"Where am I?", he asked his angel, and then his memory
served him. "Oh, I am in Languedoc, am I not? I fell off the cliff,
didn't I? I am not in heaven ,am I"? She tried to calm him.

She wet the hem of her dress and touched his cracked lips . Her
face and touch were calming to him. He was not so frightened then.
She spoke to him in another language, but he knew it. He even knew
the dialect. It was Occitan, the local language of Languedoc, of
Occitania. "Lie very still, Father ". she said in her soft accent. "You
have several injuries and should not move just yet. Your ankle is
broken and the other leg is twisted under you. You have many cuts
and some are infected. I do not know how long you have lain here and
I will have to go for help."

He began to panic. "Oh please, no! Do not leave me here

alone!" he exclaimed in French with a few words of her dialect

scattered in . "Try to drink again," she said , and he did. The life

giving water was helping. He could not take his eyes of her as he

drank. "Where am I? Are you her? An angel?" "I am not an angel,

Father, I am Merena. You are safe here. This is God's mountain."

His throat was so dry and scratched he barely could croak out

the words, " God's mountain?" She smiled, rubbing some life into his

cold hands, "It is Bugarag. Bugarag mountain, but all around here

have always called it God's mountain". It is sacred to us. Perhaps it

will be to you as well, Father." This stranger , the enemy, was not in

good shape. He could die within the day without help, she thought, but

what could she do? They could hardly survive now. The others would

be fearful, they would not understand. But she understood. She knew

what had to be done, what she must do.

The old man shook his head, "God's mountain, you say?

Then , indeed he has brought me here, and brought you to me. You must be an angel then, and God will bless you for it, Mademoiselle."

She brushed the dirt off her long threadbare skirt and handed the water bag to his good hand. " I must go quickly. It is not far where I must go, but you need medicine, food and I have to get you off that damp ground, Father". He shook his head." I am no priest. Once ,long ago, I was, but for many years I have been only the simple monk you see before you. My name is Simon, and who is it God has sent to me on his mountain?"   "As I said, my name is Merena. I live here on the mountain but I must go for the time grows short until nightfall." She plaited the fronds of three large bushes over his head to block out the afternoon sun. " "Drink all the water, I will bring more, and try not to move, Father Simon. I will not leave you long." He watched helplessly as she moved through the tangle of woods above her as her long reddish gold hair snagged in the bushes as she went. She brushed them out as she moved along. He hoped his angel would return. Otherwise he was doomed to die alone on this mountain.

Chapter 4

Bugarag mountain, Corbieres mountains, 1254 A.D.

The group of women stood around a large central campfire
some one thousand feet higher than the steep plane Merena climbed.
They were talking in two and threes as water boiled in a caldron in the
middle of campfire. Three makeshift lean-to's with blankets over the
wood served the twenty woman and two children standing around the
fire,below the cave that kept them hidden and warm on cold and wet
days. They were listening as an older woman spoke when Merena
came into camp and told of the injured priest who called himself a
monk.

The older woman spoke in low, shocked tones. "Merena, you
cannot bring this man back to our camp. You said he wears the brown
robes of a Franciscan monk, you said you saw the cross around his
neck. If he comes here he will bring death to all of us! Will you doom
us to torture and death? He will surely bring that. Besides, we have
not even enough food for us, and that only with your foraging, how
can we help the enemy? Does he know we are here?", she continued
in a worried voice.

Merena listened as she gathered her own blanket and two
others to use as a litter to move the man off the ground. "He does not
know we are camped up here, but there is only one thing I can do ..
He is an old man, Sister Garnier, very ill. I will not let him lie there

and die. I must stay with him alone then." Another woman spoke,
"You are the memory keeper and you feed us but that does not give
you the right to risk our lives. You have seen how the Church turns
neighbor against neighbor, how they torture until they hear what they
want, and then kill everyone. We cannot take a chance with this man,
he is one of them."

    "It only takes one person to be tortured and name others,even
if they do not intend to." the elder woman stood with her hands on
her hips, her long skirt and apron dirty from the fire smoke. "You of
all people know how close we are to death as they killed your mother
and father when you were just a child,we are all on borrowed time
here."

    Merena continued gathering items as she talked. The woman
threw up her hands, "I cannot argue with you because you are correct,
doing the correct thing, but I cannot agree with it either. How will we
eat if you stay with him? What shall we do?"

    Merena faced her," I understand how you all must feel. I will
only take this one small pot and some of my herbs, and stay I will
with him until he is well enough to go down the mountain himself. I
will not bring him to our camp, but I must take these items with me to
care for him. I must ask your indulgence in this matter. He is a man
of the Church but he is also a man of God and I will not desert him. I
will be gone until he is healed and then I will lead him away. I will
also harvest and forage and leave it here for the camp."

    Several women grumbled and then quietly excepted her

decision. The elder woman filled a stiffened rabbit hide with a large portion of the soup from the cauldron and handed it to Merena. "You will need this for yourself and the man then", and hugged Merena. "You are quite right, he is a child of God though he may be as poisonous as a snake. Beware he does not turn and bite when he is healed. You will be on your own with him."

Merena smiled at her, this woman she totally respected. She left, taking the broth and all her items in the large gathering bag she used in her daily foraging of plants and herbs. She must not hunt today but tomorrow she must use her wits to find food for the many who depended on her. At least they were good cooks as long as they had herbs to throw in the pot. Elder Rachelle hugged her quickly as Merena grabbed some old rags made from aprons discarded years back, and ran into the woods. "I will be back with food tomorrow." she called to them.

CHAPTER FIVE

1254 A.D. Bugarag Mountain, southern France

The old man's face was in the sun when she climbed down
to the thicket he lay in. He had been able to raise one hand enough to
hold over his eyes, but she could see the little brown trails of tears
that had rolled down the dusty face. He opened his mouth to receive
the water from the new hide she held to his lips. He motioned with
the free hand that it was enough. "Oh, my child,you have returned!
Bless you !" he exclaimed.

"Have you much pain?," she asked. He wiped tears and dirt
off his checks. His white beard covered the remainder of his old face.
"It has been rather bad but I have been able to bear up thinking you
would return with help, of course I know you were sent by God so
that helped". He looked behind her, "So who is coming then?"

Merena thought he might be just a little out of his held from
shock and the sun so she just began unpacking her supplies to do what
she must. "I will make you something for the pain, and when it helps I
will make you something stronger to fix your leg. The ankle seems to
be broken."

He watched as she went through a bag of what looked like weeds and plants in her knapsack. "You can do that?" he asked, "are you a doctor then, so young too?" She was busy crumbling dry leaves and mixing them with a small amount of water in a carved wooden bowl. "No, I am not a doctor but I know how to heal the body with herbs from the forest. It will be alright, there is no one but me anyway."

"I see" , he said, watching her mix the potion to her satisfaction. "I thought you might have gone down to the village for help, I know it is a long way, for I came up it." She shook her head, "No, I could not, how is it you are this far up the mountain and away from the village?" she asked carefully, listening to his strange accent. He drank the bitter potion she held to his lips. He started to choke from it and she gave him water to wash it down. I should have put a bit of mint in it, she told herself, but next time I will.

When he stopped drinking he said, "I am looking for someone." Merena's stomach jumped and a feeling of panic came over her. "You can talk later, right now I have to set your leg and clean out those infected cuts or you will not be looking anymore."

By the time the potion had started to ease his many pains Merena had made a small fire to boil water. As it heated she tore a small woven blanket piece into strips, then took the same bowl and mixed up a thick paste. "What is that?" he asked. She had said nothing as she added more ingredients to the paste. She showed it to him. "I am making a poultice that will harden very shortly so I need to get it on your ankle. This will be painful but it must be done or you will not walk again on that foot. You will have to hold your robe to the side so I can put it on the bare leg and foot."

She handed the hem of his brown robe to him, up to the knee. "I will have to press on the leg so can you hold this piece of wood in your mouth? And do not move..." She kneeled with her knee lightly pressed on his lower leg and turned the ankle as gently as she could. Simon jumped, and his face broke out in sweat from the pain of it even though the potion she had given him was working to relieve the worst.

She lathered the mixture on thickly and began tying the strips around it. Then she laid a small section of hardwood on each side of the ankle , wrapping tightly with one long strip she wound around the foot and heel. She tore the strip into before she reached the end of it , took each end opposite ways and tied it tightly at the front of the foot.

She had kept her knee pressed against the leg to hold it in place. As she moved it the old man dropped the wood out of his mouth and let out the breath he had been holding. "It was just barely through the skin so that is good", she said, more to herself than him. "You might have a little limp, but I believe this will heal. I have used a salve of comfrey root and yarrow,also the saints wort and some goldenseal. My clay mixture over that will harden and hold the bone in place. You'll have to stay off it for some time. And I have saved some of the potion for the pain. It's all I have left until I can gather more plants so I have to save enough for the wounds on your back and legs. But first, we must get you off this damp ground or nothing will help you. Drink the remainder of the potion and You will begin to feel less miserable in a short while. "

He looked at this girl, this angel and how easily she cared for him. "What is it that takes the pain from me? he asked. She pointed to some plants in her lap and roots in front of her. "When ground up these plants and seeds end pain, if they are used in a certain way. One has to know how to use them or they can kill". His eyes became fearful of this strange girl who saved him. "How would you know all this?" he asked. She looked up at him, "I have had to know these things a few years." was all she said., washing the blood out of his beard from the cut on his chin.

She spread another blanket on top leaves she had gathered. "Can you help me get you on the blanket? You push up and lift the good leg and I will lift the injured one. Put your hands down and push up as we do."

Somehow, they managed to get him on a good portion of the blanket and then she pulled and tugged on each end of it that had scooted under him. He was exhausted from the ordeal of it all. She filled her smaller bag with leaves for him to use as a pillow and put it under his head.

"You rest for a few moments while I clean those cuts and then we will turn you and clean the ones on your back. It must be done,Father Simon...? Is that alright to call you?" But he had dozed off with the potion,and exhaustion. She loosened his robe to his shoulders to wash the dirt and rocks embedded, then began applying salve to the cuts. He was past caring for the moment.

The Church's cross was around his neck on a leather thong but there was something else hanging there. She picked the object up and saw it was a tiny golden ring with a red stone that covered the top of it. It was hanging on a very thin leather string with a length of dirty blue ribbon on it. 'How very odd' she thought. But then her mind went back many years. Many years ago to a time when she had colored ribbons just like this one. But that lifetime was gone, and with it ,her childhood.

Now she was eighteen and the only world she knew was on this mountain. Now she had this life, and it was up to her to help her group to survive . A never ending daily job. But they had been doing as well as they could, until now.

When he woke she was gone. He saw that she had emptied her large bag on the ground by the fire. He saw packets of large leaves of wrapped seeds, plus blankets and rags. She had also left a wooden cup by his head . He knew, instantly, it was for him to relieve himself. and the water bag within reach. He painfully reached for both. It was just in time,and then he drifted off again, helpless but for the girl, and being in God's hand on His mountain.

CHAPTER 6

Corbieres mountains, Bugarag Mountain 1254 A.D.

It was dark when ,again ,he wakened. He was warm with the
blanket that had been put over him but he felt the renewed pain . He
saw the back of the girl huddling over the lit fire pit she had dug, her
hair sparkling like flames as she stirred the pot.

　　She turned around, "I imagine you are quite sore; hurting
now,it has been a few hours." He nodded looking around to see a
blanket covering the tops of the large bushes they were under. He
thought it must be her own blanket as this was all she had with her.
'She is not going to get help', was his second thought. ' Surely she
could have climbed down to some village by this time. and yet she
had not. She was certainly capable it seemed,but a broken ankle, a

physician would certainly be needed to mend that. And much rest for
his old bones.'

The smoke was filtering out around the edges of the blanket,
which was a good thing, he noticed. "Look to your right there,'" she
told him. The wooden cup has your pain mixture. Go ahead and take
it now so you will feel a bit better to eat. Tomorrow I will make
more, you have one small amount to get through the night, Father
Simon". He drank the draught, gladly.

"Remember ,I said I am only an old monk now", he told her,
"you musn't have false ideas about me, and I musn't have them about
you, surely. Were you now able to go to the village as I slept?"

She arose then pointed to a second old bowl beside him. I
must get a few more sticks of wood to keep the fire going. We still
have some cool nights here in early May. You must need to use the
old bowl. I will be back very shortly, we must get some food in you,
it's been days, and I can see your skin is getting slack. I will address
your question soon enough". She walked from the camp, and indeed
he did need to relieve himself very much.

"I found a few marron nuts around the tree with these
branches. These will go very nicely in our left-over stew." She said, "
I mostly like to throw them in a fire to roast but these will give a good
flavor in the broth when chopped very small."

They were chestnuts, he saw, and he knew them very well.
The monks roasted them on winter nights when they could find
enough for all of them. "Oh yes! they are good indeed. They grow

aplenty in England- perhaps Englandia to you" he said. She nodded, and filled the other good bowl with the stew she had created from lentils, wild onions, some turnips from her bag, along with the rabbit meat she got from one of her traps.

With her spices and herbs it made a flavorful and healthy meal. She had taken the other rabbit to the other camp higher. That and the supply of turnips and herbs would feed the others very well. They knew how to use spices by now and they would have leftover stew for the next day,mainly because many of the older women had never been used to eating meat. They did not kill, nor did they eat anything containing blood in the way they loved and worshiped. But that was when they grew their own food many years ago. In desperation they did now, of course. They had no choice. It had kept them alive many years now so nobody fussed about it any longer. Life was much different now.

She handed him a spoon of broth with the stirring spoon. "Let us see how you do with the broth first, it may be too rich for your stomach. " His pain was starting to leave, all but the ankle , and the hot broth made his insides turn and gurgle. "Oh! so good!" he exclaimed. "I don't think I've ever had as good.".. She smiled. "Wait until you taste the stew,a few more spoons of broth first though." His head felt dizzy now with the potion and the food. In fact he felt quite well. She took the bowl and filled half of it with the stew for him. "I can feed myself", he said eagerly, and did.

Not a word passed between them as he ate and she busied

herself with crushing more herbs and a piece of gnarled bark. "You'll
have this later in a tea with some Chamomile and mint. He had
started eating slow. He ate faster and faster until the bowl was empty.
"I think that is all I had better have, but I would love more. It was
delicious, and to think you made it here on God's Mountain. The Lord
certainly does provide, does he not?" he smiled in contentment. She
shrugged., "There are many who think that , I guess, but I have not
since I was as a child."

He studied her ," And how did you learn what to do, how to
find the things you do, how to put them together like that, and how to
be a good enough doctor to fix me up? Is this why you did not go to
the village to get a doctor?" Her mouth was tight. "Well there is no
doctor around here,not for a great distance, so you must do with me".
She handed him the tea and drank some herself.

There was a silence but for the small fire popping. Then she
said," What is that ring about your neck? It is very pretty but so
unusual to be worn by a priest, oh I forgot, a monk. I will still call you
Father because of your age, Monsieur will not quite work for a monk,
anyway".

He smiled, "How long have you been up here on the
mountain?, " he asked gently. She put sticks on the fire and dipped a
few spoonfuls of stew in her own wooden bowl. "It has been many
years now" she said eating slowing," since I was a child" ". And who
taught you how to take care of yourself?" he pressed on.

She wiped out her bowl and went back to the herbs she was

crushing. "It is time to change the bandages on your back , it must be done two times per day with the small amount of medicine I have. I must go ahunting tomorrow to get the things I will need. And of course we must eat. We have this stew but what of tomorrow and the day after? It must be done, and now that it is May I can get most of what I need."

" Last month we would have been in a bad way." " Well, Merena, I think you are wonderful to take care of me and I will make a bargain with you, I can see you hold many secrets. I would like you to tell me those secrets, and if you do I, in return, will tell you about the ring I wear and why I am here. Wouldn't you like to know why I climb so far up a mountain, have gone so many years, so many miles, and to know who I looked for in that time?"   Merena smiled." You might be the last man I would ever trust, Father Simon, I can only say I will think on it."

CHAPTER 7

1254 A.D.,Outskirts of Toulouse, France, The villa

However this secret and commendable Order came into being, I know not. But I have poured over the early archives often enough to know these mysterious men have always known the cruelty and injustice of the world that exists, and have some kind of hand in changes that need to be made. If it becomes a different world in the future it will be because of them.. and if this is to take place in the future I feel the Order will make the truth of the past known, and will have an influence in that happening. They have not flinched from the years of horror as I have.

Sometimes I see some action come into being that looks as if the Order has brought it about. Changes happen. however small, some months, and even years, after they have received my master reports. I notice this and wonder how they did it. And yet, the big changes don't happen. These reports also lay in the archives so they will also read and know these words I write, now, for the reader. Only time will say whether they have allowed them to be known.

I cannot know or imagine the the impact on a reader in your time, in whatever time. Perhaps the truth has already made a different world. It may be a wonderful world instead of the times I live, but then it may even be worse. The fact remains a thousand years of truth is recorded under solid rock of this villa. It weighs heavy on me to read of those past times. Nothing much has changed unless I do not know of it. It is a remote and somber life I lead here.

Men are still killing men in the name of their gods. I must eat a steady diet of this ,year after year, and I must do nothing. In these files I am bombarded with these murderous and foul acts month to month, year after year. Could you sleep, you of the future, if you knew of the evil of men in high places? If you knew the dead hearts of soldiers who kill for profit daily? I think not.

Think, if you will, of my outstanding men of the Order who read these reports each month. What must they think of their fellow men, fellow soldiers?And the many men who come from other lands with foreign tongues and murderous agendas that are sanctioned by Church and by law? Oh how they must stagger under the weight of it, and try to move mountains to leave some kind of lasting impact for the next generation to follow them. There are hundreds of events and stories, even in this age, from country to country, village to village. It is the cruelty of the Roman church its inquisitors and executions, its broken bodies and burnings.

It is the men I know who sign the documents that I must officiate and stamp for them. It is the lies of the churchmen to add to their quotas in their reports to higher ups. It is in the accused, arrested, and frightened people who are coerced to point their fingers at neighbors, as well as strangers, in order to protect themselves and their families, only to be victims anyway in the grand scheme of the Popes of the last century... And is it a grand scheme, indeed, as lands and crops, legacies and monies are are forfeited to the Church and to greedy hands before it reaches the coffers that demand it. On a signature whole villages may be wiped out on the lie or suspicion of someone.

Armies are led to murder on these lies, and the bishops and clergymen are perhaps the biggest liars of all, because they lie to themselves that this is right. Many are quite zealous about it. Even if they may not be, quite simply, they do as they are told .

Gnostics, the list goes on and on to all and any who do not fall under the good graces of the great umbrella of the Church.

This awful burden I have tried to put on you here must cease, or you will pass it off as the ravings of a demented man. But I am not, though I make no wagers for a year from now. I will go on to describe the inner workings of my days and nights and how I might think of them as my contribution to the Order, instead of bemoaning not able to do anything. I am recording these words at night, on my makeshift pallet used whenever I am in the vault.

Whenever shall I sleep again in my own bed? I have collapsed in tears many nights in many years, as I read the reports lying on this pallet, but no more. There is no more time for grief. The efforts of writing this for you take what time I have left in the nights, and take precedence. If I am to tell of this time for some future purpose, I must be honest and tell it all. I must say that I have had to become a liar , in many ways, myself in order to survive the times.

Many an official has been through my doors with papers to arrest people and comments to match. What if I had not agreed with their statements? What if I had questioned their actions even when it was an old friend? Why do I not attend mass like the remainder of the town? Yet they know I must always be available for some legal or ecclesiastical work.or at least they do not question that role I must play.

I long for my replacement but do not see that I will be free of this nightmare of humanity anytime soon. It is tempting to daydream of walking away, I have no survival worries, but I am stopped even thinking of it. I would just as soon cut my own throat as let down the Order. They will know when it is time, not I. They will know when I am no longer effective, no longer trustworthy, and so I stay . And so I write this night after night in all those wee hours after reading about death. Always death.

I read   in the reports there are troubadours many places now. Singers and jugglers and magicians , puppetry, and actors of masques to entertain the common man as well as the wealthy, the kings and churchmen. This keeps the villages happy and not as apt to think of the crusade on their own people, I imagine. Though they get plenty of entertainment to howl and rejoice ,as strangers or neighbors are burned, by the dozens, by the hundreds . I am told this continent reeks from village to town with the stench of burning flesh. It is the old Roman Panem all over again. 'Bread and circuses' for the people, food and entertainment ,while their friends and neighbors are paraded and executed for their pleasure .

I have followed many families in the last forty years. Their names and lives do not follow them into history except in these monthly pages. It is if they never existed. Some bishop, some lord , baron, or soldier turned farmer owns the land they stood on. But one family,one special family has taken my heart more than any other. Taken it and broken it.

They lived years ago, and just when I thought I could put away my grief for them and go on some of their story is causing ripples in the other eleven reports. Yes, one event has a way or sending waves through land after land. I will have to steel myself every month to come in order to break open the seals of the reports. I cannot tell it in this chronicle. I know I could not bear it, but I hope against hope that, some how ,you will have known of them in your time, that they have not vanished from existence as so many others must have before them..

You, of the future, you may learn of them in your books, their goodness, their bravery, their beauty of spirit that was destroyed. I hope that someone has written of them for you, someone who knew them, and remembered that they could still have meaning through time. You see, even now it hurts me to think of it, write of it. So I go back to other work instead. But do not let this be the end of your reading for I do persist with this. I must.

CHAPTER 8

1254 A.D. Bugarag, in the Corbieres mountains

It had been a damp, chilly night but another May morning
shed its warm golden glow on the mountain. The old man saw that his
human savior had already stamped out the fire that held her pot of
boiling water she would use so many ways that day. Merena already
had left over stew warmed up for him, kept warm on the ashes. "Good
morning", she said, Here is your pain potion, that is the last of it. I
will leave you to your breakfast. "

"Today is a foraging day for me. I will help you sit up, and
then be back in a few hours." Simon smiled, about to speak, but she
had already left the camp." He looked around and there on the other
side she had left him the old bowl to relieve himself. "Ah, she knew,
that is why she left so suddenly' he thought. In an hour she was back
with half a bag of nuts of various kinds. She handed him a flat rock
and a round one the size of her hand.

"If you feel able you could crack these nuts while I am gone, I
can bake a loaf of bread in the fire with some in it. Also, good in lots
of food," " Yes, I will, the time grows long for me without you here".
"Good". she smiled, " but just rest when you feel like it." She handed

him the small pot, to hold the nuts , then disappeared up the
mountain.

Later that afternoon Merena silently arrived back in camp
with one wild fowl of some kind that she had already plucked and
gutted, and two large bird eggs. He had fallen asleep but she saw all
the nuts were cracked and the small pot was full. He had even picked
the nuts out of the shells. The breaking of sticks awakened him as she
started the fire. He saw that she had ,once again, put the largest
blanket over the bushes which stood over them.

"Hello again," he said to her, I guess I drifted off". "I'm
pleased you rested", she said," but you got the nuts ready and what a
big help, for I am tired and there is still much to do."   The bird was
put in the larger pot of boiling water before she sat and emptied the
bag she had left in camp into the small pot. It held maybe two cups of
something that looked like dirt. "This is the last of the barley flour I
ground this winter. I have to pick the bugs out of it but it will make a
very nice loaf of bread with most of those nuts in it. Then I will put
the rest of them in the greens I collected. While the bird cooks and the
bread bakes I will have to go wash the greens in a stream, and then we
shall have quite a feast to look toward to later this evening".

"You will do all that?", he said in amazement, fully awake
now. "I do not know when I have had such a meal, or such treatment
for that matter. You must realize a monk does not eat like a
gentleman, young lady. We are not Bishops, or priests of rich
dioceses. Most of us are lucky to get a hard trencher and a hunk of

moldy cheese". She smiled and continued picking dead bugs out of the flour that had ridden around in her bag, waiting to be put to use. Her smile was full and it showed a rare full set of white teeth obviously kept white by years of some kind of cleaning.

" A trench-er? I never heard of it, what would that be?" "It is a hard, rolled up piece of bread, like this," he cupped his hands to show, " the people, those that can afford to have it, put food or meat and juices in it, and then eat the trencher when it is softened by juices" "Ah! What a good idea!" she exclaimed, " we shall also do that, but tonight you are a gentleman then, no matter what, and I am a lady, and we shall eat well, just as if we had not a care in the world."

" There!" she said as she poured the flour from her apron into the pot with half the nuts. "The bread will be hard to chew, just as the trencher you speak of,, but we will have a a thick stew of fowl before I am done that will soften the bread, and be just the thing to eat our stew with, besides you need to eat well to heal, you know, it really does make a difference in how fast someone gets well."

He studied the girl shaking the flour out of her long mane of strawberry colored hair and thought how much she reminded him,...but no, he must not get his hopes up after all this time..."You cannot have learned all you know alone, you cannot live alone on this mountain, surely...", he said, not realizing he had said that out loud. " I owe my life to you, even each day as I cannot move. Surely we are friends enough by now to tell our stories? Merena...it means 'from the sea'..does it not?" "How would you know that ?" she asked. He smiled, "Latin, I taught it to young ,would-be priests for many years. They say that is where Mary Magdalene came from to get to your land here" , he tested her. "Surely you have a story to tell."

Her smile vanished, "You owe me nothing for helping you but your silence on that matter", she said ,none too kindly. And the bushes swayed in the Mistral wind under their blanket with in the silence that followed, until Simon pushed himself up to a sitting position. He made eye contact with her.

"You know, there is probably not a secret in the world I have not heard ,and have not kept in my job, and my life. I do not believe you would have to worry about your secrets, and I might be able to even help you. Why not give it a try?" Tears formed in her eyes and rolled down her cheeks as she kneaded the small, meager lump of dough that would be their bread. Finally she looked at him, " I could never tell you anything because you are an enemy!"

He nodded his head in understanding. "I thought as much," he said gently, and I will make a bargain with you, I will tell you why I am here and if you still feel that way I will never ask you another question. Will you agree to that?" She shaped her bread into two small round cakes and said nothing.

In an hour her stew was done, her greens washed and cooked, her bread baked. Her efforts from her exertions and skills, and his appetite were each rewarded with a satisfied and delicious meal and the promise of leftovers to come. The bread, baked in the ashes ,away from the searing flames, could have been less hard to

chew and its flavor could have been improved with a bit of salt she
failed to bring down the mountain with her, but all in all it suited the
hungry bellies and the thick soup of the fowl better than if it had been
brought straight from the King's baker himself.

When Simon the monk leaned back on one elbow he rubbed
his full belly through his rough brown robe. "How is it you can do this
much with so little?" he asked. " I had a mother once upon a time", he
mused, " we mostly had porridge in the morning, and a kind of a
pancake made with drippings of bacon my father ate ,later in the day.
We were rather poor so my brothers and I left home early to make our
own way. I made my way to the Church. .. Anyway,we had brown
bread, but it had very little taste and mostly just filled our stomachs.
Here, on the other hand, in the woods, and scrub woods they are, you
can make a feast like that every day." She shrugged, "Many times I
can not! I cannot take credit for what has been put here on the
mountain, only for finding and using it however I can." Old Simon
smiled at her. Now was the time.

She was gathering the dirty bowls to take them to the little
stream that was starting to become smaller already in the warmer
months. "Please sit, and let that go for now," he said, "I want to tell
you about a girl very much like yourself, and about her grandmother
who taught her the things you know, and about her son who became
Jongleur, the storyteller." Merena gasped when he said it. "I know of
him! I have heard of the Storyteller all my life!" she exclaimed, and
dropped the bowls she was carrying in her surprise..

Simon sighed , a breath of relief and happiness escaped his lips through the white beard. . He was here, finally. It was all worth the years of hardship, of exhaustion, of failure, of leaving England for this mission of ...what? This is the moment that summed up his life.

He had almost been sure but not until he said the name did he know. And then he went on, "Yes, I imagine you might know of him, and through him I know of you and your people, but you may to decide to tell that after you hear how I know him... A priest cannot marry ,you know, although many have acted like they were. Many have not married, yet have children. I never did ,but I consider Jongleur to have been my son because I raised him from a seven year old child, you see. "

Merena sat cross legged on her blanket listening intently. 'What can he be saying?' she thought, 'he is our enemy and yet...I feel not much fear, for the first time in my life I am almost not afraid.' " It is a very long story that I will try to keep short for you," said Simon, " Jongleur's family were from here, or I should say were from not far from here, in Provence. Jongleur's Mother was called Emmalena, after her grandmother of the same name. But I knew her grandmother as Old Lena. She was a very old woman by then, and she knew all the things you do , only more of them."

" I think she could heal with her mind as well as with her potions ,but that is just my thinking. I know that Emmalena could heal with her hands, whether she knew it or not. But I get ahead of myself here...Grandmother Lena, her son in law Anton and, baby

Emmalena were helped out of Gaul,in my country we call it France,
by a Templar knight,a soldier knight from England, and a fine man he
was. The Templar knights were against people killing their own
people; many of them secretly helped them with money, by hiding
them or helping in ways they could to get them away from the
Churches armies. "

   "Strange, isn't it, with them being Christian warriors?"
Merena's mouth was open, eyes unblinking as his tale went on. " This
knight was important , Sir Geoffrey of Somerset was his name.. He
and his fellow knights were on their way to Jerusalem to fight the
infidels, to protect the holy land, when a bad one riding with them
saw a girl in the woods. He tried to meddle with her and fought with
Sir Geoffrey about it. Then he killed the girl before Sir Geoffrey
could stop him. That was Emmalena's mother and Lena's own
daughter. This young woman foraged in the woods just like you, and
just like Old Lena before her. They called themselves the 'first
daughters' after an ancestor long ago. Before the girl died she told Sir
Geoffrey where her family was beyond the woods. He promised her
before she died that he would help them, for she told him about her
baby.".

   "What was her name?" Merena ask eagerly. " Old Simon
thought a minute, "Why, it was..it was Willow, I almost forgot, so
many years ago!" he scratched his head, bald but for the little white
hairs on each side of the lifelong tonsure, however , he had a full
white beard. " So" , he continued, " he had his knights take them to

south England and gave them money, he was quite wealthy; only serving the Church at the demands of the English king to send troops."

" But I must say King Edward was all for it as he was a very pious man" he went on. "He would have done anything for the Church. So. there in that area of southwest England, in Britain, they stayed; selling the things they foraged, or made, from village to village in safety while the baby grew up to be a young beautiful girl like yourself. Now what happened, do you think? This is an awful part I must tell you.. .now Emmalena loved their life of traveling; loved outdoors, but she had strange gifts that could not be kept hidden long."

" Like her grandmother, she had gifts of the mind, and hands. She did wondrous things and could have even been a great lady as Sir Geoffrey wanted her to be, but something terrible happened to her then. The cruel knight who had killed her mother lived not far from her home village. He saw her and watched her even though he knew not who she was.. When he found her alone he attacked her; abused her, and then she found herself with his child."

He saw the horror on Merena's face. "I told you it was awful," he said shaking his head. "Now they could not stay there so Old Lena took her to a big market town, Bristol, and there they lived until the baby was born ...you see, the baby became Jongleur! And he had the same red hair as his mother, only a darker shade. And after all the 'first daughters'. he became the 'first son'. Could I have some water from that hide,please?' he interrupted himself.

She sat down closer, in fact, right in front of the old man on
his blanket. She stared intently as he drank a long drink and put the
wood stopper back in.   Darkness was creeping up on them. While
Simon caught his breath,. Merena saw the fire was starting to smolder
and hurriedly added some sticks to it. She looked up to make sure the
blanket was covering the thicket of bushes they were in ,behind two
big trees thick with leaves. She also saw that the smoke wafting out
from under the blanket was blending into the mist of the mountain. It
was an old habit. It would not do for the countryside to see smoke or
flames on the mountain.

Simon was animated now that he had a captive audience.
"They were happy there; did rather well in a market booth in that
town's large market, so well that monks, like myself, came to
them ,and other market stalls ,for items we needed to survive. Poor
monks like the Franciscans had no other way. You would think the
Church would have provided for us, but they foisted us on the people
of the villages in exchange for our prayers."

" So that is where I met them, and the clever four year old
child, Jongleur ,who told me I would be put in a small monastery in
the country in charge of building it, and educating young monks.
Somehow he knew I had rather a rebellious nature when it came to
talking with with my superiors."

" And one thing I did not like was begging and taking items
from people trying to better themselves. Poor people, ever poorer

from the demands of the tithes to the Church, and the tax to the king.
But enough about that. Jongleur's Grandmother lived in fear of the
Church due to her life here in France, for she lost many people here
including her husband. Hundreds had already died, maybe thousands
by that time. "

"This did not stop as by this time the inquisition came to
England, yes, all those years ago it raged as it does now my young
friend. I saw them again when Jongleur was about six years old and I
saw that he had strange knowledge and ways just like his mother, and
grandmother. I felt compelled to tell them in case something he did
or said with create suspicion of them. I could tell Old Lena was
grateful. She gave me a wonderful potion for my stiffness during
long prayer. and it lasted me a great while until she sent more. Then
when Jongleur was seven the end of their happy time came."

" Jongleur's horrible father found them there and tried to take
the boy. He brought the law on Emmalena and called her a witch.
She was put in jail. In the meantime Old Lena send the boy away to
me with their good friend, Louis. He was not seen, and and brought
Jongleur to me in the country."

" It was a desolate place for a small boy to be but he did well.
His mother was burned at a public stake as a witch, and. his
grandmother had threatened his wicked father with poison if he tried
to find Jongleur. He had a son six months older and they looked alike
but Jongleur would meet him many years later. " Simon was
breathless as he relived that time. He sighed at his rapt audience.

" Thinking of those years never got any easier with time, but these events must be told."I kept Jongleur away from the Church as his family would have wanted. He studied as he got older and learned all I had to teach along with the young monks I instructed, He learned but he did not accept the dogma of the Church, and he was my best student. You must understand , Merena, that Jongleur was very different. He knew things before they happened. He had visions of unknown times. And he was well aware in later years of his family and there struggle. He was well aware of a different religion than the one I taught, and why so many of his people were in danger and dying. "

"   I had great hopes for this boy I raised away from the world and grew to love, but he left me when he was barely seventeen. He had known for years what he must do. All he needed was money, and that came to him with the death of his great Grandmother Lena. The money had been saved for him; had come from a knight who fell in love with his mother. As it happened that knight was the son of Sir Geoffrey who was the one who got them away from France in the first times of killing.It was a time of strange coincidences."

"You see, it was the fourth crusade, a continuation of the Church hunting down heretics, taking their lands for the Church,paying the armies, and hiring mercenaries from other countries. They came to kill for the spoils promised them, and for complete absolution from all sins before, during, and after their service, You see, It was a free ticket to Heaven they were guaranteed." He rubbed his aching head. " So you know that Jongleur came to this land and found the people his family belonged to. Your people."

Simon was silent a few moments while she thought of all he had said. He watched the moths that flew in and out of the little camp underneath the blanket canopy. Like the people of these mountains they knew they were close to the flame , they could turn and flee only to burn up in another fire, he thought. His foot was throbbing. " I heard of him many times, and then we heard no more",Merena said , a small voice in the black night . "What happened to him?"

Simon drank, again, from the water bag.. These were the hardest words to say of all of them. "Jongleur had many adventures in this land. In the four years he traveled back and forth in these hills and mountains to bring a message ,a tale of death, but a message of hope to his people. I have no doubt that he saved many lives in that time. That because of him there are now survivors scattered to the four winds." She pointed down the mountain. "That is another name this mountain has...it is called the crossroads of the four winds!" "He smiled, I am sure you have felt the wrath of all those winds." He went on," I wish you could have read about Jongleur's family in the long chronicle he sent to me from the jprison, the same prison in which his precious mother died."

" Yes, he came back to find the man who fathered him and caused so much misery. His own half- brother killed their father,and Jongleur was arrested for it. When they found out who his mother was they gave him no trial, they tortured and burned him just like all the others. Jongleur , my boy-is no more."

He could see her teary eyes in the firelight, and he wiped his own eyes with the sleeve of his robe. He could choke back the worst of it . It had been ten long years since, and he had traveled to this land. All those long years choking back the grief of it. Heavy indeed, had the years been on him living with his own personal guilt, and the knowledge of generations of deaths his brethren caused.

He had prayed for Jongleur and the many others who died, not the prayers of his religion he knew so well, but his own beseeching prayers for all those souls and suffering, and all that still existed. It was hard to begin his story again but the old priest knew he must. It would be a long night.

CHAPTER 9

Corbieres, Bugarag mountain, 1254, A.D.

"I doubt you are aware that Jongleur went to Montsegur in the last days until it fell", Simon again began his tale. "The second Sir Geoffrey was with him, and died there. Such a brave and loyal friend.

Sir Geoffrey held off the onslaught so that four of that hounded mass
of Cathars on the great pog could escape with some manner of
precious treasure. I know not what it was. Because of him they lived to
go on." Merena listened intently as she stirred the waning fire. She
was a child when this happened, she realized.

"After Jongleur's arrest he was able to smuggle his entire story
out to me with the last coin he had, some of it I knew, most I did not
but in it I saw the sacrifice of that family, that special family. Their
good friend Louis called them his angels; what I saw and read sums
that up for me."

" Have you guessed why I am here yet?"he asked her, "why I
have traveled so far, so many years?What my mission is?" She shook
her head, "I cannot imagine, but I would like to know.". I can tell
you more if you will but answer one question for me...are you a
Cathar? Is that why you hide up here so far from society?"

She looked down, everything depended on her answer. Their
very lives depended on it. What had she brought unto them?...And yet
here was the enemy telling her of his sorrow, telling her of the hero
Jongleur people had talked about all her life. Finally she looked into
his eyes. We might have been at one time, now we are just a group of
women who must continue in hiding. There is nothing left for us. No
families, no home, no property, no future. They have mostly killed
everyone,we do not know who might be left for it has been many
years and we are surely forgotten by any of our brethren, if any exist,"
she related sadly."

" The others still practice some of the old ways, it was their life, but I have few memories of my family, just of being terrified all these years." He could see her pretty young face harden in the firelight. "And yet you have come, a priest, an enemy. And I know that if you expose us we are dead because I have finally failed, I have trusted the first person of my life and have made a deadly mistake by healing you."

"No , no, no!" he exclaimed. "You have nothing to fear from me.. I have come in peace. I have told you I am not a priest any longer, but I still am a man of God. These terrible things have been done in His name, shameful things done by greedy men with an agenda. I suppose I might have been one of the enemy at one time, but no more,never again. I can only think of the needless, heartless sacrifices and the absolute value of lives, no matter who they may be."

He scooted himself back to lean against a stump she had moved to the end of his blanket bed. "I am here these ten years on a mission,Jongleur's mission. A journey he asked me to make, his last wish in life. I could not refuse after all he had been through, after all he told me as he waited to die. "It is not likely that I would endanger this mission. So it is not likely that I would do anything to endanger any of his people. And that means you and yours. I know all about this last fifty years of the inquisition, what I do not know is who you are ,personally. "That is what I want to know. and if we can end this distrust I can discuss more important business with you. And if I am wrong I will leave here when my leg is better to continue my journey as long as I may. Shall I go on?" Merena handed him the wooden cup of pain potion she had been mixing as he spoke. " I expect you will be needing this about now,it should take you through the night, and it will work faster if you do not upset yourself. If you mean to continue you must have a heated poultice for your back. Scoot farther back , here, let me help you.... I am heating this cloth full of herbs I have collected. The heat will release what is in the herbs gradually give you some relief . Do you feel it cooling you already?"

"Yes. how is it hot and cool at the same time? It gives me relief". She sat down, "It is the Pennyroyal in the sack of herbs,that is a kind of mint that cools and works well with other herbs. We do not eat that kind of mint , though. Go ahead and talk, before you know it relief will come." She helped him find a halfway comfortable position.

"You do beat all", he smiled at her showing discolored but a healthy set of teeth, "a nurse, a doctor, a cook,...everything a young man needs for a good wife.." "I'll never marry", she said immediately, "and I'll never have children for them to kill in front of me."

He patted the small hand that put the heated pad behind his spine of sore bones and joints, "Perhaps it will not be that way forever, perhaps you can go away from here."

"I told you I am in a group. They have been my family in these years, I could never desert them." He nodded, "So commendible...and do they knew I am here in your care?" "They do, Father Simon,but they will not see you there,you must understand why with all their losses, all their fear." "I do, child, I most certainly do,..so you go and and forth between the camps?"

She threw more sticks on the small fire, "Yes, I took them the other fowl, the greens, some nuts. They also have a storehouse there-what remains from winters use. We are all very self -sufficient as a group. If we had not been we would have perished up here, It still would have been better than perishing down there."

My back feels much better, what else is in the poultice you made, if I might ask?" Merena had taken the poultice to heat it once more. " It has many plants and herbs in it,mostly I use the same things for inside or outside the body. Elderberry... most people do not know that a supply of Elderberry should be kept at all times. It can cure almost anything if one knows what to do and how to use it. I use all parts, the leaves, the flowers, the bark, and the roots. Good for boils, infections, I used it on your cuts, for swelling in your back and leg,for coughing illnesses,, for fevers of all kind."

" Now that it is spring I can find the white blooms. And , even more, it also can be used to dye clothing and make ink. And that is just one plant of hundreds. White willow bark, evergreen oak, mint, holly oak, elms, nettles, rosemary, thyme, poppies, dandelions, and many other flowers. The woods, though not so much the scrubby ones you see here, are a market of food and medicines. I only wish I knew more."

She took a deep breath after all the words tumbled out of her.

Old Simon shook his head sadly, "And yet, the world does not learn these wonderful things,you realize that this is one reason they accuse women of being witches and burn them? And yet there is nothing evil about it, just the opposite!"

She watched him closely, "Did you believe this at one time?" He shrugged in response, "Many things are in scripture, some easy to believe and some not so easy. You must remember that most of the scripture we know was written by man, and as we see, man is imperfect. Men make many mistakes saying this is true or this is the way it should be. The most powerful men are the worst because they make the rules for the rest of us."

"Man would not have been given a mind at all if he had not been meant to use it and decide for himself. I think that is why I cared so much for Jongleur, he learned, and made up his own mind. I was the same when I was young, I must admit, and had to spend many hours praying for my own guidance. Man has two feet to stand on, Merena, but when those feet trod on others; then they become feet of clay. They are doomed to collapse when all others with two feet stand up to face tyranny, when they stand up to be counted. Jongleur knew this from an early age. He made a difference, he stood up. "

He became silent, gazing into the fire. Merena sighed a deep sigh. "The last thing my father said to me before he died was 'If anything happens to me you find the storyteller and you will know where to go. I was twelve. People talked about him in meetings, about finding him, but there was no way to get out of here. Father told other stories he had heard on long winters nights."

" When they dragged Father away to question him the elders
came for me and ran to the caves. They knew he would not be back;
that he would be tortured but kept alive to burn in public . They took
nothing, they had nothing. Men went down at night to get food from
others who had not yet been named or suspected. Also for items that
could be sold, but that became too dangerous and many did not return.
If we had met up with any groups leaving, I am sure they would have
taken us. There were men among us but it was a struggle to feed all
the people every day. Most went for food and never returned. They
found that my father and others were tortured before they burned them
in the village square. We are eighteen women still, and the two
babies that lived are eight and ten now."

"And what about your mother? Simon asked gently. "She
died when I was ten", she said.. "It was in childbirth and the baby
also died, but she carried too much fear besides the baby. She had
time to take the consolamentem, and I got to talk to her a few minutes.
In those minutes she tried to tell me something but I could not
understand her words. She went out of her head and died . The other
women have said my mother became very afraid that we would all be
taken, that is one reason she kept me with her in the woods. She never
told me anything of her family, even when I asked. She smiled, " One
good memory I have before then is when some of us children used to
play games...we used to tie a blanket or an apron around our necks and

pretend we were the Storyteller. We would twirl it round us as we told a story just like the messengers said he did. He became our hero, our hope for the future".

Father Simon listened intently, "How is it you knew how to forage in the woods but the other women did not?" She shrugged, "As I said my mother took me from the time I could walk, but I have learned many things right along these years, the times to plant, the times to pick, but my mother taught me as soon as I could talk and repeat back to her. I spent every season in the woods with her. She used many things she found, and then we also had a vineyard where she learned everything that could affect the taste of our wine."

I don't know how she knew things. The elder ladies said my grandmother died before I was born. I remember one of the elder ladies saying my grandmother knew all these things too when she was a girl. She was the first to come here and she brought the 'memories' with her. She said my grandmother had a sister somewhere in Provence ,but that my grandmother had married a man from the summer meeting. He moved them here to his land and grandmother never saw her family again. I never knew her. but I have always felt her with me, even more than my mother."

Merena quieted and stared at the fire for awhile, lost in the few memories she could bring forward. "Mother was the memory keeper of my people. She awarded that honor to me before she died even though I was so young. She pointed at me and said the words once more before she died. This is the one thing I understood because I had heard her speak many times in our meetings. And her grandmother was a memory keeper before her so I guess it was passed down."

"And just what is a memory keeper?" he asked. " She put the reheated bag behind him again, "Well, I should not tell an outsider, it is in our religion, our legacy. I will only say that it is an honor to hold it. Women are very important in our religion, and in each family. After all, they bring life, sustain it, and enhance it . Unlike the world we have seen where women are ill treated, we consider their person to be most valuable."

Simon was more and more curious, " And when would you have seen this mistreatment since you have been in hiding these many years?" " I was twelve, as I said, I guess I remember these things from that age... after all, in your world that is almost a woman, to be married, bought and traded by rich or poor, like part of the cattle, I have heard from the others." He nodded sadly. "You are very wise for your years."

Old Simon laid down and began thinking as she watched the silver mist move over the moon he could see beyond the blanket flap hanging down. 'Perhaps he was wrong, this may be just another pocket of people desperate to survive all these years later. They were certainly still being hunted. He knew for a fact that four years ago the Count of Toulouse had gotten another Bull from Pope Innocent to root out heresy.

In the years he had walked in Provence, and now in the Languedoc he had seen the push to rid heretics and separate them from their rich lands. The last Count of Toulouse, Raymond Travencal had submitted to the crusaders and the new Count. He was more than a Cathar sympathizer but his daughter married to the new Count was not. She had been raised at the French court in preparation for her marriage to him, the brother of the king.

In the last years the Inquisition was back in full force. Old Simon new that all the action was within a weeks distance of this area if an army had been sweeping out of Toulouse and down to Carcassone. He would be helpless to do anything but bring more death to these people unless he left as soon as he could. But first he must be certain about this girl of the mountain and forest, this child that had been through so much herself.

Chapter 10

Corbieres Mountains, Bugarag

1254 A.D.

Merena left him the next morning after filling the water
bag for him and heating the remainder of the leftover stew. "I may be
needed most of the day, today, since I have been gone a few days.
Also, I need to find more food and leave them some,but I will be back
before night fall," she told him. "Do not try to put any weight on that
ankle, it would be a mistake, I will leave everything in your reach."

" The air is quite nice today", he said." I will be fine if you
take that blanket off the bushes".   She left him then, and began her
climb further up. Their camp was situated in a pocket between a
house- sized chunk of limestone and an an area maybe ten feet higher
where the caves lay in the upper mountain. The recess protected them
from any view and against the cold winds of winter and the oppression
of summer heat. With a three foot climb an entire view of the valley
always was visible.

It was a five minute escape to the caves if need be. She had
checked her primitive traps before she went on up and found two ill
fated rabbits . They would make a good dinner with some stored
vegetables in camp. In the last seven years she had made a summer

garden and a winter one here on the upper plateau. These small sized
gardens she beganfrom plant seeds recycled. from the year before. The
garden below and camp above were hidden behind the scrub bushes
and trees; and the soil was covered between seasons in case the
inquisitors sent soldiers up the mountain. That had never yet happened
because they could see miles from the caves and lookouts. When
groups of men on horses were seen in the distance they headed to the
caves right above them. There were many who went with
Merena ,deep into the mountain ,where no man was likely get through.
They had planned well, a few of the caves had a storehouse of wood
and basic foods like nuts and plants that would keep them alive in
bad weather. So far no heavily laden soldiers or pack animals had
even attempted anything but the base of the mountain in passing by..
They had both winter and summer camps on the far northwest face of
the mountain where climbing was nearly impossible ,and no villages
in view that could see their smoke.

"I am glad you are here", said Elder Garnier as Merena
gave the signal and walked into camp. "I was worried for you, and
today is meeting."
"Yes, I am here and have brought rabbit today. Should be a good meal
for meeting." Elder Garnier took the rabbits, and smiling took the
girl's hand. " Ah, thee never fails, we are very lucky to have thee.
How does your patient, the priest ,fare?" " "I think he will heal", she
said, "but it will take time to knit that ankle, he must be able to walk
on it. He is a very nice man, Elder Garnier, he is no longer a priest
but a common monk, he says. Not only did he know our Storyteller,

but raised him from a child. The other women quickly gathered
around . It was a name they all knew. " This monk is looking for
someone ,but he has not said who that is. He tells me the Storyteller
has sent him." At that there was an excited tittering from the women
who knew the stories well in those earlier years ,when they held out
for hope. as they froze and starved.

"The Storyteller no long lives", Merena said sadly," Those,
who are our hunters, have killed him." A loan moan escaped almost
every mouth and Elder Garnier bowed her head, "May God hold him
close for the life he lived". And silent prayer descended upon the
group.

Merena sat down on her pallet and dumped the contents of
her forage bag to sort out what she would leave in camp and what she
would take with her later. While the women cooked the meal, she
made a bowl of balm to divide within the two camps. There were
always injuries in camp. Cuts, scrapes, burns were a daily occurrence,
so a supply was always kept on hand. Likewise, a supply of potion for
stomach ailments, and general maladies was always needed. It all took
time to crumble, grind, mix, and store in their utility area, out of the
weather. There they kept the dried plants, herbs, roots. and meager
vegetables from there small garden of the season. Nothing was
wasted, even the rabbit skins were saved and scraped to hold what was
stored, or kept the two children clothed and warm as they grew.

A few of the others knew how to use most of the herbs and
spices ; some who had gone foraging with her. In time Merena .

even discovered that there were salt deposits within the mountain. which she chipped pieces off and stored. Not only did it make food from the woods taste better,it extinguished fires without using precious water, cleaned dirty pots, made winter ice walkable, killed weeds that might hold, mosquitoes or snakes close to camp. It even lessened sore throats and if sprinkled on greens so they would not wilt.

"Shall we go to meeting while the meal cooks?' said Sister Garnier, "I think it is a day to give thanks for our safety, and our wealth of food today".

It had not always been so the first couple of years. Merena was young, winters were hard and there were so many other people then. Babies died because their mothers had not the health to produce milk. Illness was constant. One by one the men knew they had to leave to find food. There were exceptions, but one by one they failed to return and hope was shattered. They had only their faith to keep them going. Somehow they survived until Merena made her self remember what she knew but had banished from her mind from terror.

The strongest remained alive and as scrub gardens produced some food the women used all their skills to make it edible. In these years Merena was the blessing that kept them all going with her knowledge of herbs and medicine, and with her ability to find food. The fear of the Church's discovery and torture was uppermost in the mind of each of them, but they went on; heartened by enough to eat and the prayers of their faith. They gathered,led my Sister Garnier.

She was the leader of prayers, the parfait of the faith, and the woman all looked to for her spiritual purity. After her prayers and words each of the group was to say what she wished, her own prayers, concerns, and suggestions.

They sang their songs of praise and hope. None hoped for their old way of life. That was gone; would never be again. Now they simply hoped for survival even though their faith was based on the death of the body; their spirits longing, and belonging to God. All their emotions were audible in those songs of praise. Desperation, fear, love, faith, and hope.

On a very windy day those raised voices might have been heard as far away as Couiza . Surely the cattle shepherds they heard singing their beautiful chants at nights may have heard these heavenly voices and wondered if they were angels. Perhaps they were never heard, and endangered by the hunters ,as they were in their cathedrals and churches singing or listening to their own choirs of a Sunday morning.

Elder Garnier spoke , "Sisters before we have a closing prayer it is time we honor the memories of the strong women before us whose lot was much worse than ours could ever be. Let us hear from the memory keeper, who follows a long line of memory keepers so that our ancestors are never forgotten, our women of grace,and we never fail to think of their sacrifices." Merena cleared her throat to begin her litany of the women of the past and their contributions. This , above all, was her contribution to the group; had been since the age of ten, since the death of her mother. It was a legacy she was very conscious of having heard her mother speak every week since she could remember. It was passed to her, just like the knowledge of the forest. It was up to her to honor those important woman for all they had been Her voice rang out in a clear, pure tone.

"All woman in name who lived before, whose blood we share, and who live in lore,

We honor,remember your works and lives, how they helped God's word survive,

Across the waters to this fertile land, with sons and daughters in their loving hands,

The Sarah's, Maria's, the Martha's we adore, the Tamar's and Miriam's ; so many more,

Namesakes, daughters who bred us all, from dusty Palestine to verdant Gaul,

Who held the truths we live to pass on, who gave us strength to face every new dawn,

The caring of Ruth, the strength of Tamar, and shining Stella. the bright morning star,

The Naomi that lead them with wisdom true, our teacher Magdalene,we honor you

Joanna's devotion, with each saint we rally, to keep kin close to heart within this valley

The Bethany's and Anna's gone before, with each sacrifice you opened the door,

    Wherever we flee, wherever is home,

    each beginning has duty of its own, each daughter must
guide ,prepare our way,

    To give us courage for each new day

    Our harvest,more than food, for we have sacrificed many,

    None so great as our Magdalen, she suffered more than any,

    We honor her in all women since,

    Her love was greater than any she need repent,

    Our men who tried to keep us safe, have now passed through
Heaven's gate,

    And of those who strike us down we must love, not hate,

    For each who burned are more than ash, they need no flesh
and bone,

    They suffered from the sword and lash, but the spirits live in
their Father's home.

    We who remain must pass a test that others have each done,
Then the time will come for eternal rest and until that time has
come.

    Each women in time must be our guide, on she has the inner
know,

    To pass on our ancient's pride, to help each generation grow,

    Matilda's, Hagar's, Esclaramond too, give us grace to cope,

We know of Juditha and how she could heal, And the messenger
Jongleur if , indeed, he was real,

The enemy surrounds us, as in times of old,Yet they cannot erase
each spirit we mold,

Each generation goes to Glory for their lives, loves, and
deeds,

They sowed the seeds of Earthly life, now we must water
their tree.

There was a moment of silence, as always, to show respect of
all the women who had come before including the unknown nameless
ones lost in many generations. Elder Garnier lead the last prayer
knowing that someday her name might be on the lips of some other
memory keeper, or be one of the nameless through the ages, held in
such esteem. It would be enough for her.

The oldest of them, Sister Legasse, tapped Merena on the
shoulder as the girl rose up from the stump she had found to sit on.
"Do you remember hearing much of anything else about your
grandmother.. did your father know her very well?" Merena shrugged
as she braided strips bark from the stunted trees above them." I have
been thinking about her lately. He said she was a fine lady. That is all
I know" Merena shook her head, " I know mother learned the woods
from her."

Sister Legasse smiled, " I thought of it when you recited the memories, I remember when she came here to the Languedoc with her husband. I would see her at the yearly meetings. People came from all over the area, you know, to worship together. I remember her saying that Juditha was the memory keeper, and was her grandmother back in Provence. Also that Juditha's oldest daughter was her cousin ,the same age as her, so her mother was your mother's aunt, but she had not seen any of them in many years. "

"Your grandmother married very young, then came here. I guess I remembered the name Juditha because it was different. It must have come from the Judith in our scriptures. She and her husband had met at the yearly gathering where she came from.", repeated the old woman. Merena was amazed, "So our Juditha of the memories was my great- grandmother?" she exclaimed. " What an amazing thought it is to think my family was so honored. ' it gave being the memory keeper knew meaning to her. '

Yes," the woman commented, "I suppose that is why you are the memory keeper, it was passed down the line, and that is why it was your mother, and now you." Merena looked startled, " Perhaps that is what my Mother was trying to tell me before she died".

'Sister Legrasse went on, "I am sure it was not known, may be not even by Elder Garnier. I have not thought of it in years. Our people just knew the memories were always passed down in the meetings. Someone special was always the memory keeper in each generation, and it kept many of the names going, but surely not all. There have been too many generations, some must have been lost with the people.in time." Before Merena could think any more about this new information, Sister DiFalga called those gathered to dinner, and as they ate their greatest interest was about the old priest who was not a priest. Why had he come? What could have enticed an old man to climb a wild mountain? How could the things he said be believed?Where was his family?

Merena answered each query as best she knew how . "He has not yet told me why he is here except he looks for someone, and he was sent by the storyteller before he died. It is such a sad business. Perhaps it is someone who can help us if he was sent to find him."

They commented to each other, all thinking of the possibilities. "I will bring his words back to you when he is ready to tell them. We must realize he is in dreadful pain and has sustained many cuts besides his broken ankle. I have done what I can and the pain medicine gives him some relief. He is quite elderly so he tires so easily. I must say, he has a beautiful speaking voice, and his accent is so interesting and odd. As I said, he states he is from the Englandia. He says it is a huge island in the North Sea, surrounded by water, yet it is not so far from France, which we know is what they now call Gaul. Still, he is hundreds of miles from there and has been on foot in this country many years."

She was ready to leave, looking for the things to take to the lower camp. They were all watching with interest as she rolled up her pallet stuffed with gallium and woodruff. Elder Garnier came to her

with a rough carved wooden bowl of the rabbit stew they had made.
"This is the last of the stew, take it to your monk who is not a priest.
He will need good food to heal. "

Sister Garnier turned to address the group of women
beginning to do the camp chores. "We can take a vote if you wish it,
but I think I can speak for everyone . You may bring your old man
back to our camp when he is better if your judgment is that he is no
threat. Perhaps he can give us news of the outside world, and can
advise us. We cannot stay up here forever. We are all thin in spite of
surviving this long, and what of the two children?"

The others nodded and became animated with their own
conversations. Sister Ranierd came forward with a shawl, "Shall ye
give this to your monk, the nights are still chill." Sister Navarre
approached, "I see you take your pallet , why not take the one that
belonged to Sister Lagarche? No one has used it since her death and
surely it would get him off the damp ground."

Merena smiled at all of them. "You are all too good,.. le
bon femmes..., I know Father Simon will be so grateful for these
kindnesses." She left them with her arms full, saying " On the
morrow I shall return with whatever can be found. I have taken a
handful each of our Haricot beans , and lentils. If you will boil up
the remainder in the bag I can predict we shall all have a kind of
cassolet tomorrow, and it is time for a few cattle or goats to begin
wandering. We shall soon have some cheese , I am in hopes," she
smiled.

CHAPTER 11

Bugarag mountain, 1254 A.D.

Old Simon was straining to look out on the beautiful
valley through a hole in the bushes when she came into camp. The
cattle chanters, shepherds, were calling in their herds for the day.

"Their voices and chants are lovely, are they not?" she said in
greeting. "You can hear them across the entire valley", he exclaimed,
" I never get over how they sound like a chorus of angels, the way the
voices blend. It seems they call to each other... there is exquisite
music in the churches too . I wonder how those choirs would sound in
this valley, that would be like a choir in Heaven. But these are
gladdening to the heart too."

He was happy to see she had returned for it was a lonely

sound that echoed up the mountain, as well as an angelic chant. "I do
not know where I have ever seen a more majestic country, or such
music that could make you weep," he said. "They have kept me
company these many years as I walked from village to village, but I
imagine you have heard them all your life."

Merena put her bundles down and sat by his blanket. "But I
never get tired of hearing them," she said, "Soon it will be time for
stragglers in this spring weather. I watch for them and when there are
two or three goats or cows I have my pot ready to claim a little of
each ones milk. No one misses it and we can make a little cheese to
have with whatever else can be found."

He smiled broadly when she told this. "You have had to be
very brave indeed, in every way, a little mother to your charges, even
to thievery." She shrugged, "No more than the others, they've had to
bury their own children, and friends. I am up here as a criminal
anyway in the eyes of their Pope." He patted her shoulder, "I guess
that makes me a criminal too, for I have found favor of your
company. and your plight."

She reached for her bundle of items and the pallet. "See what
the others have sent you, a soft mattress stuffed with gallium, some
call it Lady's bedstraw. It smells like fresh hay and honey, and now
you will have a softer sleep. Elder Garnier has also sent you the
leftover stew from today."

He took the bowl handed to him. "I am so pleased! And
lovely in smells, Your friends seem to have trusted that I will do no

harm, it is very kind of them for as little as you all have." He began eating as his mouth watered and the aroma coming from the bowl was too much to resist. "It's easy to 'magine," he said with his mouth full, "what these ladies could do with food in their homes." Merena watched him enjoy his dinner. "They have also said I could bring you to our camp when you are able to walk a little. I did not think they would hear of it , but I think they are starved for conversation; starved for news of the world.."

" He stopped eating for a moment."I am so very glad, I knew the exact same feeling. But for the campfires of your people from time to time I have been walking alone for these ten years. I have been too many places to remember."

The cattlers chant was dying with the light of day. It would be a warmer night and no doubt a beautiful moon. She had rolled him to one side off the blanket and then back onto the pallet with he blanket to cover him as needed. They both lay on their soft pallets looking up to the starry sky.

"When you get better," she finally spoke, "I will take you to a spring of very warm water and it will help the foot heal faster." "Yes?", he said in a surprised manner. "And it can heal? I cannot remember bathing in heated water for many years, never when I was young or at my little teaching monastery. Oh how wonderful it would feel on these old bones! But how did you find them?" She smiled, " This area has many such springs if you know where to look, even on the mountain. There is fire in the mountain that heats the

water. you can even find it coming out in a stream as you sit under it.
I have found one fairly close. I watch above the stream, and we go in
twos on Sundays sometimes. We all look forward to it but it must not
be when activity is near. In those times we use a cold stream or
pooled area up here."

He was full of wonder at this girl who knew so much. " Have
you been down into the mountain?" She shook her head, "It is very
dangerous, I have been in some passages that go down a great way
into the mountain, but they are steep and it is too dark. There would
be no one to find me if I fell , or was lost .And then what would
happen to the others?" "Yes, of course you could not risk it," he said ,
chewing on a piece of the fragrant straw that poked out of thin
material of the pallet.

He was pondering his next question to her, finally, " We have
not spoken of it; I wonder if you had any thoughts yet of why I am
here?" " She shrugged, only that you have some mission, but why
would it lead you to a such a place as this-a wild mountain? Perhaps
the caves?" He went on, "Have you any knowledge of the names I
said to you? Emmalena? Old Lena, Willow? I know you have
Jongleur." he finished. She shook her head. "How could I have
known of them so far away?"

He laughed, "Right you are", and what about "Esclaramonde,
or Lissamonde? Juditha? Lorelei?" She sat up on her pallet. "Who are
these women? How would you know of Juditha?" He smiled at her,
"Ah, so you know of Juditha, not a common name is it?" A big sigh

escaped him. It was time , after all, he was finally here. She was who
he had come to find. But he listened.

" I told you I was the memory keeper, the names of our most
important woman who we honor. Juditha is one of them!" He could
see she was excited, "I imagine she was" he said, "Juditha was one of
the 'first daughters', a bloodline that began with Mary Magdalene", he
said softly. "You see , Juditha was Old Lena's mother, and the others I
mentioned were, after her, all 'first daughters'; all committed to
memory except the ones that were lost to the ages."

She just sat shaking her head. "That is not possible, I would
know it,someone here would know about them if that was so..."
"Merena, someone obviously did know it, but they might not know
more if they were being protected. If none knew it around them, or
within a hundred miles. Then they could not be tortured for the
information, could they? For centuries the bloodline, the memory
keepers, the first daughters had to be protected for the line to continue.
Otherwise how would you know the name of Juditha from five
generations ago?"

Merena was up and pacing now. He saw the beads of
perspiration on her forehead as she tried to wrap her mind around it. "I
do not see how this can be" she said, "one of the sisters in God, the
oldest, just told me she remembered the name from the memories. she
said my grandmother's mother was Juditha. This Juditha was part of
the family left there and she never saw them again. She had a sister
there, I know. I never heard of this before, these people or a

bloodline. It is hard to even imagine such a thing."

Simon nodded, "I know, but you must try. This is your family, and after all these years I have found you, for Jongleur. The women I told you of are your aunts and cousins, Jongleur is your cousin, was- I mean. He wanted me to find any family of the bloodline, any 'first daughter' to continue the line, and that is you. It was your mother before you, and your grandmother , and all the others."

He took the ring which was around his neck and handed it to her on its threadbare ribbon cord. This is what he wanted that person to have; this is what he wanted them to know." She looked at it. "It is a ruby," he told her,"you see it is in the shape of an egg. This belonged to the Magdalene and it has been passed down to each 'first daughter' to continue the line.

Juditha was one of many, but the first I know to have it, then her daughter Old Lena, then Willow, then Emmalena, and last -given to Jongleur when he was seventeen. Each of them helped their generation in many ways, were many things to many people. They were seers, teachers, healers, medicine women, and foragers."

" Jongleur led his young life for his people, I believe he would have been a great man who would have made even more of a difference in this world, had they let him live. The egg was Mary Magdalene's hope of a rebirth ;of the way people thought, that there would be no more killing; there would finally be understanding and peace and tolerance for all people. They all wore it. Jongleur wore it as he traveled here to help his people,now it is your turn." She shook

her head in dismay. " Even if I believed this about these relatives,

about our Magdalene, I can do nothing . You see how it is, how it

has been for generations. I would not be deserving to wear it,I am no

Jongleur." "Oh, but you are", he disagreed, look what you have done

already at your age-how old are you? I figure about eighteen or

nineteen....look how many you have helped, what you know; I would

guess that you know other things you would not admit to right now."

" I imagine it comes into your head to mix just the right things

together, that somehow you know yourself, where to find the items .

And you are the Memory Keeper, you have kept it going, just like

your mother. It could have ended with your mother, yet you, like her,

kept it going in the worst of circumstances. I wonder what other

memories have you blocked out from fear? What other things have

you seen in the past that have happened? You told me yourself that

you knew to hide in the wine cask, as a child until the right people

came, and the soldiers never saw you. You found me here when no

one else could have. Something led you to me on this mountain. And

none of these things would have happened if you were not you. The

one to carry on the line." He shifted himself on his pallet as best he

could for his many aches and pains. "The other women honor the

Magdalene, but you continue her. Her blood courses through your

veins just as the very first daughter, Sarah Tamar, the princess.

You are the next descendant to pass it on." The old man laid back, his mission finally done. He was exhausted in body, and the effort of the explanation, His mind was full of the years of travel in all weather, the miles walked, the questions asked, the scarcity of food but for any monastery he passed.

She sat gazing into the fire, numb in body and mind. This made no sense, someone would have known, would have told her , surely, if any of this was true. Her Mother would have, wouldn't she? Would not Elder Garnier know something this important, this life changing? And what about father? Yes, she knew things,she always had, but they all had different abilities, did they not? But he was saying she came directly from our Mary Magdalene and...who? ! The Jesus in their scriptures? Yes, I guess our brethren and sisters believed that they were a couple, in some way, but this was too unbelievable, too personal for her. And yet she could not deny the stories of Jongleur and his gift of knowing claimed in the stories about him. She looked at her hands that had treated so many injuries the last eight years, and yet she could not save some lives of her people in these years. Why not? If she was a healer that didn't need medicine? She knew when the hunters were coming, knew when it was time to hide them from view, from discovery,but that was all. And even if it were so what difference did it make? People were still being tortured and killed. And the women are still in danger.

"You are mistaken, Father ," she finally answered. "I am not the one Jongleur sent you to find, there must be another who can do more, who deserves the honor and can wear this ring. When you get better you must search again , It is not I."

She turned over on her side to go to sleep. He just smiled. "Not you, indeed? You think you have not done enough to be the next 'first daughter'? You have kept yourself, and twenty other people, alive for eight years when thousands of others have been rooted from hiding and been exterminated. This is more than Old Lena, Willow, and Emmalena could do. Old Lena died from extreme old age . She did as much as she could. They gave the world Jongleur, and he made a great difference, but he had me , or he would not have had a chance. The ladies have had you...or they would not have had a chance. I call that a leader, a disciple, a 'first daughter' with super natural abilities that kept you all alive. You are mistaken, Merena, Whatever abilities you have now, or will come into later whenever you are not living in constant fear, constant work, I do not know. "

He laid   his head back down on his own soft pallet next to the fire and watched the life giving, or life taking flames. " What I do know is that, your face, your hair color, your talents, your blood relative, Juditha, are all like the others. If ever there was another link to the bloodline, another 'first daughter'...it is you. It is a family you must accept as your own. What you do with the knowledge of them is up to you."

Chapter 12

1254 A.D. Toulouse, France, The Villa

Who are you?' I lay back thinking in wee hours before the
next dawn., when I put this writing in its secret place until the next
night. You, who may read my words in another time...What must you
think of us as you read of this century of murder and torture, in
addition to the crusades of the infidels and the wars raging elsewhere.
The Church has some hand in it all, you may understand,one way or
another. If that sounds unfair consider what I say. They do affect
everything. The world I know revolves around the Church and its
tenets, its activities. Of course they demand that all people join with
their one true religion whether they wish to or not. Those are the
infidel Moslems, the Jews, the Albi's, Cathar's, Bulgar's, Lollards,and
all sects of many other names. One reason is that Church is jealous of
those tithes that do not come to them in these groups. It is a vengeful
opponent.

Most of the affected people have made a success of their lives
with land and property, and that holds an interest for many who watch.
The Church has power over the kings to excommunicate them,which
the Pope does most freely if his demands are not met. Demands that
include kings to outfit and send thousands of soldiers and knights to
fight to the death wherever he wishes them to be. That would be to kill
the infidels in the East, the rebel sects in Europe.

Those kings, such as Frederick, who are not threatened or
concerned about excommunication fight for the lands the Pope wants.
As for land. whatever the Church does not own, the Knights Templar
do, and the Church looks upon the fertile, prosperous land of the

rebels with a desirous eye. With troupes needed every year in the holy land what the Church must ,then ,do is hire these deeds out to mercenaries. It works out well , they come by the hundreds and thousands from other lands, encouraged that they not only will share in the spoils of goods and money they retrieve, they will also receive an automatic ticket to Heaven for every past, present, or future sin. They can rape, murder, and plunder with abandon without fear of excommunication for any reason; but only after they serve in the round up of all religious rebels and carry out the necessary extermination and seize the property that becomes Church property.

It is a political game at this point , who runs the vast holdings for the Church, which kings, which Counts and Dukes may collect rents, hunting rights and other benefits in those areas or countries. The administration of all this must be a tremendous undertaking. Add to it the political games of positions in the Church and in all these new lands and it becomes the largest business in the world.

If they are not already, I must predict that one day the Church will be the richest organization of the world in money and holdings, and this is how they acquired it. One would think that an ecclesiastical future would be where to make ones fortune in the world, and if you are a bishop, archbishop, perhaps even an important priest or inquisitor that would certainly be the case as they do live in luxury and wealth;having very different lives than the lowly preacher or friar.

It is not unusual for these , supposedly celibate,clergy to have large properties of their own along with wives and children, who must have good appointments for their own futures.   You may wonder why people have not revolted here against this treatment to their neighbors, to themselves. Fear is the reason. Fear that anyone could be targeted at any time. If a neighbor holds a grudge any comment can implicate a complainer as a heretic. If a husband is in need of a new wife the days of the old one might be numbered. It is a dirty business.

What I do not need to sign, I certainly hear from the men who come for their business to be done. Over the last fifty years many brave souls have tried to alter these actions, the condemnations and the burning. St. Bernard tried to convince the Pope that the Cathar's are preaching a Christian message; that they have exemplary lives and purposes. He was too important to kill -but his work continued in silence about the Cathar's.

Arnold of Brescia was convicted of blasphemy because he spoke out against the material splendor of the Church and the luxury the clergy lived in. This holy man was hounded, and hunted to his death by Frederick Barbarossa whose armies were supported by the Church. Peter Abelard was silenced as a heretic, first exiled, then hanged, burnt and his ashes were thrown in the river to join the hundreds of others who met the same fate.

These rivers run with the evidence of these times, the people drink of it. The Cistercan's and the Carthusian's maintained spartan life as monks. They speak against church policies and the luxury of upper clergy. As you understand this you might see that it is, in no way, healthy to stand against the Church, even if you are a respected clergyman in your own right.

No statements made against Church policies or abuses last long, or guarantee the speaker's health. The Knights Templar's are sympathetic to these hunted people and they, mostly ,manage to stay neutral since they are fighting in the East or tending to their banking and properties. They have their own notaries and magistrates so I do not know their business practices ,except to say that they own as much property as the Church here in France, and other countries.

I feel it will not be long until the Church has its eyes on them too. Currently they are in the East with King Louis and his Armies. I hear Brother Reginald De Vichier is now the Grand Master of the Templar's, and he has met Lord De Joinville in the East. Our Master in Toulouse, Fabienn LeBlanc has gone with them.

Meanwhile, here, the Count of Toulouse has ceded his lands in the North to the crown, no doubt to help fund the Crusade. Parliament is holding a court of investigation of our local authorities finances while nobles are not taxed at all. We remain in a system of feudalism. I have heard that everywhere one looks now resides a Cardinal sent as a Papal Legate. They answer to no one but the Pope so their activities in the local churches, and their constant investigations and condemnations are never in question.

They have taken over all local courts here, they collect all the fees for fines .What they do not keep goes to Rome, or Lyons. Such men have been in my office here to see if my fees can be extracted but I seem to have a dispensation as an important function to be provided for church and local nobles ,and have for many years. They do not leave here happy. I am ill at ease but I am eternally grateful for the protection the Order gives me.

It draws close to the day of reports for this month. I know I will have a sour stomach and mind from the days it takes me to read the other eleven. and begin writings of my own. More of what I have written will be apparent but I must save my anxieties for the one family I watch with the most concern. You will wonder how it can be followed so closely but be assured the Order certainly is efficient in all its ways.

I see evidence of this each month. It is particularly a wonder to me how this organization stays clear of the Church, yet it has these many years in all the territories which are covered by my fellow sentinels. I steel myself to do the best work I can each month, each year, in the knowledge that it may be helping the underground of those suffering, and that the Order always has my safety, and interest, uppermost in their actions.

Meantime , it is easier for me to include such areas of my Master report to the Order as you see here, instead of writing it once again. I continue to withhold other parts I know they may wish not to include until some later time they may choose to divulge themselves.

CHAPTER 13

Bugarag mountain, 1254, A.D.

Old Simon leaned on a forked stick Merena had made and
hobbled out of camp when he needed to. It had been two weeks since
the women welcomed him to the camp. It proved to be a pleasant , if
not a shocking, time for them all.

The first day he sat around the fire with them and told them
why he had come. He told them about Britannia and Englandia,some
of the younger had never heard those names, and his tale of the family
of Emmalena and Jongleur. He told them about the marketplace and
Angle, or English, peoples. And he told them about the bloodline that
had come down to Juditha, and those he knew back to the Magdalene,
all the way down, now, to Merena.

It was a shock, to be sure, but little by little it made sense
to those who had known Merena's mother long ago. Her strangeness,
her potions and herbs, her fear of discovery. Simon told them what
he had seen in his years of walking and searching, the many burnings
from villages to towns, most by the Church; some by villagers who
formed mobs. Yet he had seen such other inhumanity that there was
no way he could speak of most of it. He had never known men to act
that way, he had been sheltered but for Jongleur's story.

It took hundreds of such men for every order passed down by

the popes, archbishops; most of all, the inquisitors. The screams of terror, the horrible tortures, the rapes, the digging up of hallowed ground to burn bodies, even after they were dead . No , he could never speak of it. in this company.

In fact he had to work hard to block out such scenes from his mind, from his dreams. He no longer prayed about it, no amount of forgiveness was possible for the things he saw. Had people gone crazy? It seemed so. And now he was here with these good women who undoubtedly would meet the same end if found. It was intolerable to consider. And what of Merena, just when he had found her in his last years? Nothing he could do would save them. They must know it, and yet here they were taking care of him. Kind attention he had never had before... he must not be more of a burden but what could he do? Only wait until he could walk, and then, what?

They enjoyed the old man's stories and news from their own county, even where they had lived. He certainly enjoyed the new attentions of the many women as they brought him comforts that were the few they had, and fussed over him after they knew him better.

The work for Merena was much easier now that she had the one camp to forage for, and others to cook. She even had time to watch for straggler cattle, and goats grazing on the mountain. With her two pots she stole a little milk from each of them,not enough to be missed, though it seemed to her that there were more stragglers this year, the shepherds must be getting lazier in their work.

Now they would have a small cheese, a little butter, and a

bit of milk for the two children who were undersized. The girl and
boy were fascinated with the old man, who told them many stories of
his adventures, and some that Jongleur had written in his chronicle.
They had heard all about the hero, Jongleur from the womens so they
were thrilled to meet this man who knew him.

Simon's ankle was still far from being healed. He could not
step on it yet. Sister Authie, who cut all their lean-to posts, and who
made the bowls and cups for each of the others, went to him with a
gift of a beautiful walking stick made from some hardwood. She had
hand carved it during many campfires, not saying what it was to be. It
was carved with angels and polished with the fat she could beg from
any game in that time.

She had spent hours chafing her hands as she massaged a
golden color into the cane using her own body oil. The old man was
speechless when she gave it to him. "All I can say in thanks is that I
will treasure this the rest of my life," he told her, wiping a tear from
each eye. Elder Garnier lead the clapping of the other women when
he hobbled on it. "Such a beautiful walking stick , it looks like
buttered molasses", she exclaimed. The two children just stared at her.
They had never seen molasses.

Merena cautioned him not to use it until he was more healed.
"As soon as you can put weight on it we must get you to the hot
springs; the healing waters will be very good for that foot. I think it
will make the difference whether you limp or not, so no weight on it
for a time. The pressure would stop it from healing right."

She tied his leg up so he could not step on it when he
hobbled out of camp to relieve himself. It was untied again when he
sat on a stump, or laid on his pallet. "It is too tempting to put that leg
down, or even stumble," she told him. "You will not be able to go up
to the spring we use, we will have to go down to one by the river. It
will have to be on a Sunday ,so two weeks from today should be about
right. Sunday because all people are in church all day.".

        Simon's pallet was put in Merena's lean- to, made like the
few others, from short trees, interwoven branches and leaves sealed
with clay earth to form a roof,plus more brush piled to form three
sides . The open door was covered with clothing or their blanket in
rain or cold.

        . Woven branches formed the floors which were then covered
with the bedstraw, gallium atop pine branches. The scrub of the lower
plateau made for good coverage, some of it was hauled to the upper
plateau since more coverage was needed to protect them view. The
camp went about its daily routine but it was greatly changed around
the visitor in ways that concerned the women.

        Old simon had never been used to the ways of any women, so
he was never bored as they washed and hung clothing, fixed whatever
meals they had, sat talking about their lives around the night fires,
organizing their religious meetings. Besides talking to them as they
worked he kept the two children entertained about the lands he had
walked, stories of the Templar knights he had met, and the animals he
saw in his travels. He also taught them a little of the

English language ,and tales in the books he read.

Those days were pleasant for all, a temporary relief from the drudgery and fear that had surrounded their lives for many years. In the nights after the fireside fellowship he retired to Merena's enclosure and they talked of Jongleur's family, and his travels. They also talked about Merena's healing gifts of knowing the right potions and poultices to use as she changed his bandages. The infections from rocks and dirt on his body had been healed in very short order, the ankle needed more time. She had made the other aches and pains he carried for years almost disappear with different potions she made.

He felt better. It was not easy to talk to her about her feelings as hers had been so suppressed many years. Gradually, she came to trust him and tell him of other sensations that went through her mind. The knowing of what others of her people had been through, the feeling she had to climb to the window lookout of limestone at the summit, only to see vast numbers of soldiers miles away and which direction they were heading. This meant doused fires, decisions when to approach the caves, and people to alert.

In her times of sleep, images of another life called to her in her dreams. One where she walked barefooted in hot shifting sands, another where she sat at the head of a tribe with other women who wore colored robes of purple luxury, and taught men, as well as woman. She washed away these dreams each morning with the dew on her face, for only real life mattered, as fearful as it was. As they fell asleep to the chanters heard over the valley, and dreamed of families that were no longer there. No one dared to dream about the future. Each day was a struggle, and it was all each of them had.

CHAPTER 14

Toulouse, France   1254 A.D., The Villa

My future reader, if you are still reading, I must tell you all.. Toulouse and Carcassonne are in an uproar the last few days. I am brought much gossip, and much paperwork, to take up my daily hours. Some of the bringers are almost cheering, while I see fear in the eyes of others.

Pope Alexander has just issued a Bull stating that a new Inquisition , heavy with torture must be initiated in all of Italy immediately. Of course that news will spread through France rapidly, especially in the mind of the inquisitor in Toulouse, Bernard DeCaux. He is best known for bringing the 'Edict of Faith' to this whole area. Not only must each person sign a document declaring the Cross, they also must confess any knowledge of anyone else that may be a heretic. This may be any blasphemous curse word, any suspicious activity, any word of gossip uttered about another person. All must be reported.

DeCaux is also known for his administrative genius in filing all reports by name, and cross referencing every comment made by each person. Then he can go back when he sees the slightest discrepancy and recall anyone he wishes for interrogation, as many times as he wants. The inquisitors simply say it is all one time of investigation with repeated punishments if necessary.

He has demanded entire villages to be interrogated, one with over five thousand people. In Toulouse's jail at this moment are two hundred nineteen adults, and eighteen infants , all have not passed his interrogation methods. These are awaiting some final tribunal, or death after punishments of semi-starvation, shackled in dark cells, and long confinements;some to five years or more. Even those who have signed the edict are subject to recall at anytime, for any reason.

DeCaux has been here in my office twice hurrying his paperwork and messengers. I have felt the deadly stare of that interrogator , personally. I would not like to see it again,as it has been in my nightmares too many times. Yes, I have signed the Edict myself, no one is immune. Like the other inquisitors I have seen from the reports, no one undergoes his inquisition without confessing. The jails are full of those who were not guilty of anything, but would have confessed to anything. The rivers full of the ashes of the burned flow on..

An Inquisition clerk was killed by rebels twelve hundred forty -
seven. All the inquisitors, clerks and courts now must have guards,
even as they walk through villages and in the monasteries. The rebels,
who form parties , have learned that lists can be burned and not go to
the courts when the clerks are attacked. This saves lives even if they
lose a few.

There are many knight sympathizers who join them in these
attacks. Most are no threat now due to increased guards in each court
and with each inquisitor. As you might surmise, with the Church's
army, the Kings armies, and the Templar's in Jerusalem and other
infidel cities there is somewhat of a shortage of military guard since
most of the other military is busy at some battle,at the jails or
burnings.

I have just read that Templar knights from England and
Scotland are being sent to be guards in France and Spain, the heaviest
population of heretic inquisitions. This will free the mercenaries to
replace the dead. German and French soldiers are dying by hundreds,
even thousands, in the East.

Henry III is in Gascony with his brother, Robert DeSanford,
the Templar knight who is Master of the London Temple. The King
will go on to Paris to meet with the French King. Over a hundred
English , Scottish Templar knights , an d some German knights are on
their way to guard DeCaux and his Inquisition to Spain , under heavy
guard since he is so endangered between the countries.. Others will
go to Carcasonne, but the greatest number will go with him to
Spain and Italy. There he delivers the Edict of Faith.

Even though the hunting of heretics never ceased in this area, townspeople had been breathing somewhat free and going on with their lives after signing the Edict. When DeCaux returns the madness will be stronger again. Ones who have rich crops and fertile land should be concerned. The two sentinels in France must take extra care at this time. and I am the third one. I smell the fear in all our reports.

I watch a certain family with trepidation, with no way to influence. I hope the sentinels in France and Spain will be safe from the onslaught that is surely to come. Any absence of reports will tell me if they have fallen prey. As for me,   Have I lied when signing the Edict, or facing DeCaux or his men? I certainly have, and will continue to. Have I agreed with their glee at the roundups. the tortures, the burnings? Of course. If not, I would be under immediate suspicion.

This is not my Crusade. Even if I was one of the hunted this would be no time or place to stand for them, I know too much to be suspected; to be tortured. Stronger men than I have failed to resist. It has not threatened any of our sentinels so far, God willing it does not. So I will continue to fake laughs with the men who come in bragging of the conquests, or bringing papers of condemnation for my magistrate seal. I have known some of these men for thirty years, have been friends with them. I pity them for their trappings of wealth and their hearts of poverty. I have been tempted to say, 'look what you are doing, these people are the neighbors, you have known all your life for their kindness'. But I do not , and will not ,say a word. It is not for me to judge. There are lives at stake that must come before mine, above all. This time in history will pass but the Order must stand.

CHAPTER 15

1254, A.D., Bugarag, Corbieres Mountains, Southern France

June was almost spent, bringing welcome warm summer nights to God's mountain. Father Simon, for that he was called by his new friends, in spite of his protests, spent his days doing the foot exercises Merena taught him, to strengthen his ankle. He was getting around camp quite well, now, thanks to the fine walking stick Sister Authie made him, while Merena braided the stripped bark off young Birch trees she had collected in the spring. It was to be used for strengthening the roofs and sides of the lean-to's they had.

The winds and rains had been heavy in May , and all but

destroyed many of their little huts . Now, they cooked each meal during daylight as no heat was needed at night. A torch or two in camp was all that was needed.

Merena had , also,collected herbs and plants the entire spring. Now it was time for the summer ones, especially the blossoms of so many plants that would aid her potions, and even give a new taste to the food they ate. This was an important time in their survival. The Gallium shoots and leaves were added to soups. Sunflower seeds were eaten raw and in the many foods they could prepare, They could be wrapped in the large sunflower leaves with seeds and chestnuts and cooked in the fire or ashes. The boiled seeds and leaves made a potion that helped coughs and colds. She collected wild onions, and green lentils, purple Iris blossoms and their green stalks. The thick rosemary bushes were loaded with pale blue clusters that were added to stews and soup , and dried for potions. The cowslip added a sweet flavor to grain mush, and hortensis added a peppery flavor to stews. Burnet, and other greens were found for salads with whatever dressing they could make to flavor it.

Honeysuckle brought a sweetness on the breath, on the tongue and to eat, and added fragrance to the lean-to's in camp .And the White elderberry blossoms were eaten, and every other part of the plant had value. So many other flowers were available to gather now. lavender, cornflowers, tulips, roses, marigold, sorrel, calendula, violets, and even clover was edible. Now was the time to collect the inedible ones too. The important foxglove, poppy, and she used in potions .

It was her busiest time, and the other women would help to separate and store the large amounts she and one or two of her helpers brought in. When she felt like she could take a break, Merena told Father Simon it was time to take a trip down to the river and let him soak in a hot spring pool. He would enjoy it, it would help his foot, and his brown robe needed serious washing. He refused to wear a blanket while they washed it.

Sister Authie volunteered to go along and help as he would be using his walking stick and another sturdy forked branch. But the walking would be steep, and a fall would undo all Merena's work to heal him. They waited until Sunday, when all locals of the small village would be in church. Those hours there were long so they would not be home until the later afternoon.

They left in the early morning knowing the descent might take a long while with Simon, and it did. He would never have made it to the upper pool they used on the mountain, but with the women on each side it was slow but steady trek down the steep curve of the mountain. They reached the plateau and it was just a steep , rocky hill from then on.

Spring had at least given it a rich bouncy layer of grass of the season ;leafy trees offered shade and shelter from view until they got within sight of the village. Since they were Northwest of the village Merena had made a path she used for the times she snuck down for items, or to milk the strays she found. They used this all the way down to the river. She had disguised it with loose brush clumps which they kicked aside for the old man to walk over. She would replace it later so it remained hidden from view..

And there was the river waiting, lower now in the dryer season. She found the spring still gushing from the side and the round higher pool it made with its power. At some point it had been dammed by man or naturally, and was a size and depth for two or three people to sit comfortably in the hot water as the hotter water splashed over them. Later in the summer the gushing water would slow to a trickle.

They had to help Simon walk over the exposed river rocks and knee deep water to get to it, and then to climb into the pool. Merena took his sticks and laid them on the riverbank. A glorious two hours followed with them sitting in the hot saline water in their clothes. Old Simon sighed continually with unknown pleasure. They washed his head and what little tufts of hair he owned with salt water, and even the robe on him as he sank down into the water and laid his tired old head on the dirt top of the circular pool.

The two women washed their own hair while he relaxed. .It was the first real bath he'd had in a very long time, he said, only washing in cold water streams as he traveled, or ,still cold, in monasteries he came to for a night's stay. Merena knew that it was more important for him to be getting the good of all the minerals in that water. She had no knowledge of what they were, only that cuts, and other injuries, were greatly improved by the water. She allowed as much time as possible

for his enjoyment while she watched the riverbank on both sides.
Then they helped him out and back to the bank where he wrung out
the tattered hem of his brown robe.

They wrung out their long faded dresses and combed their
hair with their fingers. The two women did not put their hair back up
as it was so long their would not be time for it to dry.

Merena's hair hung past her hips in sunbleached reddish curls.
Sister Authie's grey hair was longer, even. It was thinned with age,
and from wearing it in a tight braided bun all her life.

It was enjoyment time for Simon to sit there, on the bank,
and dry off as he was steeped in sunshine, and time for the women to
see what they could find of value to take back. Before Merena left she
cupped her hands with cool river water for him to drink more of the
healthful water. The sun was hot on them all, drying them, feeling
wonderful. None wanted it to end.

Merena and Sister Authie were busy looking for trees that
might hold a beehive. Honey would be a treat to take back to the
others. They already had found a bag full of nuts. Merena scouted the
trees along the bank since they were bigger than any on the mountain.

In just that instant they did not see the procession of horses
that came around the bend of the river. The three were sighted at
once by the full range view of a hundred knights in full armor. The
lead knight, and the red- robed DeCaux in front, signaled the entire
army to stop.

Merena was panicked, there was nothing they could do. The

women tried to hide behind trees but it was too late. "You there!", the inquisitor priest on horseback yelled. "I see you!, All of you come up here at once. Do not try to run . My men will ride you down."

The women did not move. Father Simon, spoke up instead. "Your Grace, I cannot climb the embankment, I have a broken ankle that is not yet healed. The ladies are from the village and are helping me." But the inquisitor was not to be placated. "Who are you, monk"? I can tell you are not from around here by your accent."

Simon rose to the challenge, " I am Father Simon from Somerset, England. I have come atraveling to this beautiful country on my way to make a pilgrimage . I have here come from a monastery in Carcasonne if you think you have to check." he said testily.

The priest just motioned to four of the knights to ride down and get each of them on the riverbank. "We shall help you on your way when you are able." the priest yelled, "you must get to the road anyway." Sister Authie was terrified to see the knights coming down into the riverbed. She began running up the mountain to get away but one of the knights rode after her and picked her up like a sack of feathers.

A young knight held his hand out for Merena but she ignored it. "I will walk", she said to him. She dropped her foraging bag. "Let me give Father Simon his walking sticks first, he cannot be without them, you see". The knight followed behind her on his tall dappled horse.   The two other knights did not bother putting Father Simon on

a horse they carried him chair-style up the river bank , sat him down
on the path and went back for their horses and his sticks.

By the time got to his feet with his sticks, Merena was beside
him and the young knight was beside her. The knight was back with a
crying Sister Authie, her grey hair hanging down around her
shoulders and half-braided.   The knight handed her down to stand by
Merena, then he stood behind her.

Inquisitor DeCaux turned his blazing eyes on them. "Who are
you, and what are your names?" he challenged, but Simon interrupted
him, " "Your Grace, they live here and saw me fall. My ankle has not
yet healed and they helped me out of the river. There is no need for
you to detain any of us!"

"I will decide that, monk , you do not know our ways. As far
as that goes you can be on your travels, my business is with them. Do
not interfere." "Your names", he repeated to the women. "W-Widow
Authie", croaked Sister Authie hoarsely.   "I am her daughter,
Merena," said the other. " The inquisitor was too sharp for them.
"Authie," he barked, with a slow smile."That's a Cathar name, bind
both of them," he instructed the two knights who were off their
horses .

" I thought we had burned all of you in this area. Who else is
here?" he demanded. Merena looked defiant, "Sir, you are making a
big mistake, we were made to take an oath already. You are trying to
detain a poor widow and the daughter that takes care of her. We are
on our own and have done nothing."

Simon joined in," I would not be with them if they were
Cathar's, you must not add to their troubles of getting along. It is hard
enough for them. You see the rags they wear. They were out
searching for food when they saw me. Surely your men should give
them money for food instead of detaining them like this."

The inquisitor took an instant dislike to the old monk. His
eyes blazed with distrust. He turned to him. "I think you had better get
to the village church and rest for your travel. Your assistance is no
longer required, if the women are innocent they will be listed in my
files in Carcassonne. You notice this rebel vermin cannot even say
'Your Grace'? There's more to this, you should know it too, monk ... I
will delay my trip to go back and see if they have signed, they will
have to take another oath if they have, but I know the names of
Cathar's. I doubt they pass the test. We will deal with them as we have
all of them."

"Sir Reginald, ride the widow with you , Sir, ..what is your
name, son?", he said to the younger knight. "Sir David McDowell...
Your Grace", he said almost sternly." " Ah, one from the Scots land
by your accent, nice to have you with us, Sir McDowell , take the
girl. . You won't be to the jail until sometime late tomorrow. In the
meantime, I will visit the village to see if they live here, but of course
they do not. I will return to Carcassonne in two days time. Tell the
jailer he may start the interrogation, with good notes written for me."

He looked at the tired, sweating horses who had just come all
the way from Carcassonne.

"You men look for whatever shelter you can find for the horses in this mess they call a village. Then send some men house to house for food. You will have to camp in a field outside the village." The Templar knights looked none too happy with the barked orders but they were sent to guard this man of power, even so they must heed his orders, temporarily. Whatever little church was here the men would have to go ten or twelve at a time for vespers and Mass.

The two knights rode off with the women sitting astride the pommels in front of the knights with their hands tied in front.The big war horses began an immediate gallop to answer the will of each knight. Sister Authie had stopped crying and kept looking back at Merena who shook her head at her and tried to smile. DeCaux had already mounted and rode off with the other knights.

Father Simon leaning against a large rock called to the women before they rounded the bend of the river."I will find you, do not fear!" He sat by the dusty road amid the horse droppings, trying to think. He would wait for someone to come along and then he would try walking for awhile He was terrified for the women, his ankle hurt, he was hot and there was no way he could get back down to the river for a drink of water, much less thirty or forty miles away ,to Carcassonne.

The knights were at full gallop for a couple of miles and then slowed to a walk to let the horses rest from the extra weight. The younger knight called to Sir Reginald as they walked.

"We can do some fifteen miles before nightfall, is that your

thinking?" Sir Reginald dropped back. "If we keep a steady trot until
dark we may do so, have you food with you?" "Not enough for all of
us", the other said, but we passed in inn about ten miles forward. I
can get it there, and some ale. It will keep until camp."

Sir Reginald nodded and gently kicked his horse. Merena
smiled at the devoted Sister Authie as they rode off. Sir David
pushed her long flying, curly hair out of his face as they bounced in a
trot. "We will tie your hair back when I stop at the inn." he said
gently, but she ignored his words.

Two hours later they arrived at the busy inn. Sir David
dismounted and handed his reins to his companion knight. "I shall not
be long", he told him, knowing that Templar knights got immediate
service in most places

Shortly, he returned with a basket and a jug of ale on top. he
took a small dagger out of his boot and cut the rope that bound
Merena's hands. One half he gave to her, the other he used to tie the
basket on his horse. He pointed to her hair, "Tie that up, if you
please", he said politely. Merena did as he asked. She tied it to one
side, doubled the hair and retied it.

"She is not bound", stated Reginald, who did not seem to be
bothered with his prisoner's stringy hair. Sir David sighed, he was not
happy about this mission, "She will not escape on horseback, I will
retie her after we have eaten, they must use their hands, you know".
Merena rubbed her chafed wrists as they rode.' If there is any way I
can escape tonight I will find it, but what of Sister Authie? And what

of the women back at camp? No one must know of them'. Sister Garnier could take care of them for some time, there was food, and more stored. But her situation seemed hopeless.

Father Simon began walking , as well as he could. The sun was in the West now, he could a make it a few miles by the time evening came.Then he could find a church, or perhaps a house that might welcome him for the night. He must get a start at dawn. He heard a racquet and turned to see a farm wagon coming up behind him with a youngish driver. It stopped and the man said, "You look like you need a ride Father, can you get in?"." Oh, praise God" , exclaimed Simon, panting as he struggled to climb. 'Another angel sent..."

" I have never been called no angel, I am just a shepherd goin" to pick up his brother." He chuckled, " He might be an angel though, he is finished with his seminary studies and comin' home for awhile, I guess... have to go all the way too Carcassonne... the monastery, you know." "Oh," said the old man, that is just where I need to go,what a blessing you are." "I must stop at the inn at dark", the man told Simon," you are welcome to share my room and we will get an early start. My Father feeds the stock until I return, two day hence. It will be good to have company along the way."

Simon nodded, "You have just the one brother?" he asked. The man smiled wryly ." I am the youngest of four, You know the eldest gets the estate, I work for him. My second brother went off to be a troubadour, not sure where he is after being gone several years.. Then my third brother will be the new priest in our village." "I see,

what a lot of boys! So you are the shepherd?"   " Yes, I was tutored
for awhile. I sang well but the Church was not for me. I went to
University a few years back and decided it was not for me either. The
city is too dirty, too crowded, so back to the farm I came. I prefer the
open countryside." They conversed easily as he urged the two horses
along at a pretty good clip.

"I see, it is you, then, singing the beautiful chants in the
valley?" " Yes," the man said, "I sing to the stock, they know me that
way. I t could be me, but I am not the only shepherd,we all sing to
pass the time. It is a lonely life."

They stopped a few hours later. The inn had but one room
left as the room had been busy that day. It was not much of a room.
The young man, whose name , Simon learned, was Christopher. "
Simon sat in the one rickety chair that the man motioned him to. "No
wonder you came upon me", he said to the young man, "Christopher is
the saint that assists travelers!." The young man laughed and told
Simon to take the bed. "I'll take the floor" he said, I would not let my
father sleep on the floor let alone my grandfather." He made himself a
pallet on the floor and would not hear of Simon's protests.

Simon was grateful, he had been spoiled by the care he had
gotten from the women. He was not prepared for today's ordeal. ' The
women, what would happen to them? What would happen to Merena
and sister Authie.? It was a terrible fear he had for them. How
frightened they must be! He must get there before it was too late. Now
he saw the terror these good people lived in year after year. His
church had created devils that hunted down and murdered innocent

people. They had come to God's mountain today and he had seen the
worst devil, the inquisitor who arrested Merena and sister Authie.
Father Simon had heard of him in his travels. He knew nothing would
would stop him from burning them.'

CHAPTER 16

1254 A.D., Road to Carcassonne, France

The two knights made camp in an open space off the dusty
path. It was in a level circle of pines and the level ground was
covered with pine needles. There was no need for a fire on that
balmy night.They lifted the women off their horses and Sir David
tied Merena's hands back loosely. They took their helmets and
saddlebags off, then the saddles, and tied the horses to trees not far
away. They had already removed the white surcoats with the red
cross on them, and their chest armor, the hauberks .

Now they removed the chain mail over their shirts and hung it
on a tree branch They allowed the women to lean against the saddles
while they passed out mutton and bread to them. Sir David took two
wood cups out of the basket and handed them to the ladies, full of
good quality ale.

Sir Reginald had untied Sister Authie's hands and tied her to a
tree where she sat. He looked at the young knight and expected him to
do the same. " You really think that is necessary?" he said
,sarcastically. Sir Reginald gave him a scowl, "You forget who we
have here, Brother McDowell. "

McDowell persisted, "All we have here is an elderly lady and

a scared girl, aye, you forget what they will do with them", he said ,
his Scottish brogue murdering the French accent. He started to tie
Merena to a tree when she said, "Sirs, if you will help me we can
quickly gather pine boughs and woodruff for bedding, it would make
for better sleeping after your long ride. If you lay your horse blanket
atop them you will hardly feel the ground at all". Sir Reginald gave
her a hard look. "

"You help her", he said to Sir David, "tie her to you with your
reins, but be quick about it. It's already getting dark." He checked to
see the horses grazing and sat down, leaning against the next tree to
Sister Authie. She turned away from him and watched as Merena and
the other knight, as disappeared into the woods.

" I need to find the gallium with the last light that is left, but
you see there are many boughs of pine around each tree we can pick
up even in the dark. " He nodded, "What is gallium?" "It make's a
bed soft, it smells sweet", she told him. " you can even make a sweet
wine with it."

He followed her six feet behind with the rein tied to his own
waist. She found a patch of gallium and woodruff and started
gathering it in her dress. She mentioned for him to gather it too. He
sniffed it and stuffed it under one arm. "It does smell sweet, how did
you learn of it"? She shrugged, not wanting to give him any
information that would render her guilty.

"Women know many things, I think men do not choose to
listen." She turned toward the camp, "This is enough, I think, it is

darker. Shall we dump it where we will sleep and get the boughs? "
This they did in the middle of the circle of the camp. They did not
have to go far to gather up armloads of soft pine boughs.

"Where will you sleep?" she said to Sir Reginald. He pointed
to the other side of where sister Authie leaned against his saddle.
Merena dropped the load she had under each arm and spread them out
in the shape of a pallet for a tall man. She looked at Sir David and
pointed to the pile of woodruff He moved so she could grab some in
the bottom of her gown and carry it to the pallet . She spread it,even
pushing some into a small pillow mound. She did the same in front of
Sister Authie, caressing her shoulder when she was done.

Then she looked at the young knight. He pointed to his own
saddle and she made his pallet, and one beside him. "Now you must
spread your blankets over them. They are sticky if they get on you.
Please, use the blankets first, to give us privacy for our needs ,away
from camp."

The knights led each of them right outside of the camp and
met with those wishes. Holding blankets up but holding the prisoners
by the long reins. When they returned Sir Reginald retied Sister
Authie's hand's without saying a world and pointed to her pallet in
front of the saddle.

McDowell kept Merena tied to him and laid down, allowing
her to use his saddle for her head. Soon there was snoring from Sister
Authie's guard but Sister Authie lay there watching Merena, and
crying softly. Merena mouthed the word 'sleep' and soon they both
closed their

eyes. Merena waited. She was not asleep.

The young knight had turned on his side, away from her. As she waited, she worked the knot of the rein attached to her. Very slowly and quietly she had loosed it. When she heard low, even breathing next to her she began to release the rein around her waist and move. He ,slowly, reached behind himself -then she felt his large warm hand pressing firmly against her arm. She turned to the side,away from him, as he quietly reached to retie the rein and laid back down. "You know they will kill us, do you not?" she said softly, "Guilt or innocence will not matter." She heard him sigh, and then she fell into a troubled sleep."

Chapter 17

1254 A.D. Carcassonne, France, Le Mur Prison

Father Simon was dropped at the town market not far from the prison. One of the vendors gave him bread and a cup of water as he passed. He had blessed him, and the man from the wagon before he left. It was the least he could do. Two hours before, the knights had come through the gate to the prison. Merena was awestruck by the outer, and inner walls ,that surrounded Carcassonne, and the many people inside the walls. It was also a wall of humanity, it seemed, for it was more people than she had ever seen before. Sir Reginald spoke aloud. " 'The Wall,', that is what the prison is called, and where it located, in the wall around the town. In the French- 'Le Mur', " ,said Sir Reginald to the young knight as they entered. " That's what they call it, now prepare your senses to be assaulted, Brother McDowell".

They stabled the horses temporarily with two ragged youths that were feeding a few others outside the prison.. Sir Reginald grabbed one boy's arm. "See you take proper care, feed, water, and wipe him down. You will get a coin from me, or you will get a cuff."

Merena was still tied to McDowell but hugged Sister Authie
close as the knights motioned to two men busy digging moldy bread
out of a barrel, preparing to feed prisoners. The smell permeated the
air."Where is the jailer?", Reginald asked. The man pointed down the
stone hallway and said he was in the first chamber there . Sister
Authie's guard then guided her down the hall, and the young knight
followed with Merena. They all tried to cover their noses from the
assault of human feces, sweat, rancid food, a a certain other smell that
Sir David recognized instantly as old blood. He knew it well from his
years on the battlefield.

The young knight gave Merena 's shoulder a gentle pat as they
went into a large room that held another long hall filled with tiny
cells, and what was left of the people in them. A baby or two was
crying but they could not see it, or the mother. Merena looked down
the cell line. Some were deadly silent while others had moaning,
crying, and a few screams of pain. She turned to look at Sir David
with a steady gaze, but he could not hold it. He turned away to watch
Reginald walk over to a busy man with a cruel line to his mouth.

There were two burly guards standing next to the man, and
more guards at the far end of the hall. The frowning looked up and
saw them. His eyes lingered on Merena, and he smiled. Sister Authie
was now crying, uncontrollably. The jailer nodded to the guards to
take the prisoners to a cell at the end of the hall. As the women were
untied by the knights, two guards grabbed them roughly,and started
dragging them down the hall. Merena looked at Sir David helplessly.

"Hey!", he yelled at the guards, "These are women, not mules, stop that rough treatment!"

The two burly guards stopped and looked at him, eyes moving over his armor, and the long sword in its scabbard. " Knight, these are not women- they are prisoners, and they are ours now." He reached down and grabbed Merena's breast as she struggled against him. Sir David lurched forward with his hand on his sword. "Touch either of them again and I will cut out your heart! Aye, that I will!" he said. One hand was on Merena's arm, the other hand had his sword half out of it's scabbard. The Jailer walked over to the two. He motioned to Sir Reginald. "Hold your friend."

Sir Reginald bristled, "I take no orders from you!" The jailer nodded to the two guards and each of them quickly grabbed the young knight. Faster than lightning the jailer reached out and backhanded Merena, who screamed in shock , holding her injured jaw. The young knight shook the big men loose and drew his sword. Reginald had his half drawn. But the jailer stepped in front of the guards, and said with a smirk. "You have no say here, gentlemen, I take orders only from His Grace, DeCaux. Take your complaints up with him...he may think you are a Cathar sympathizer...you may wind up here yourselves. Get these criminals in the cells, guards". and they took the women away, Sister Authie shaking and crying, Merena holding her bleeding face where she had been hit by a hand with a large ring. The knights, stopped in their tracks, were giving the jailer steely looks; but they were not moving. Sir Reginald pointed a finger at him, "He shall hear from me indeed, in England I would deal with you quickly, myself.." The jailer still smirked, wiping Merena's blood off the ring he wore on that hand. "You are in France, so get the Hell out of my jail."

Sir Reginald slapped the hilt of his sword , in anger, and turned to go. Mcdowell hesitated, " I am not leaving," he said to both of them. I will wait for DeCaux, we may have no influence with him but he will not be here to protect you from my sword if you ,or your guards, touch either one of those women again, I will use it.!"

" I will call for the King's soldiers in that case," said the jailer. Sir David laughed, "Evidently you do not know that knights of the Temple have total immunity from any laws in any country. We answer only to the pope . I will stay here and be allowed to see the prisoners under my jurisdiction until DeCaux returns. Bring on your soldiers, they can keep me company."

He strode with Sir Reginald to where the horses were kept next door in the open stable. "I cannot leave and let them harm that girl, no matter what they say she is", he told him, "The next time he will do more than slap her, I saw the way he looked at her. They all may, look in those cells."

Sir Reginald began to saddle his newly groomed horse and threw the boy a coin. "Do what you must, Brother McDowell, I have to check in at the preceptory. They think we are on our way to Spain. If these heathens give you any trouble, send this boy for me. In the meantime hold your sword, and your tongue." He pointed to the stable lad looking at him with shining eyes .He had never seen one of the tall knights with their silver armor , and long swords with fancy silver hilts. The knights in their white mantles looked like warriors from Heaven to him.

Sir Reginald mounted his horse and gave the Brother sign to McDowell, who went back into the large room that housed the cells in that Godforsaken cesspool. Feeders were busy throwing slop, or moldy bread into some cells for some of the prisoners Babies still cried.. he wondered where they were kept as he walked down the length of the cells and glanced in. He was sorry he did. Some were chained in the dark and he could see they sat, or lay, in their own feces. Some were strung up by their ankles or thumbs, in agonies past crying. Some were praying, others talked out of their heads about a something called a consolamentum.

Rats kept them all company and ate the bread thrown in. Women held ripped clothes over their naked parts, where guards had gotten to them. One held a crying baby but she had no milk to feed it. Whatever they had done, surely death was better than this. He wondered why, and how, they kept them alive.

Finally he got to the last cell. Merena held Sister Authie's hand and mopped her bloody cheek with the hem of her dress. The older woman was staring as if it was all a bad dream, moaning to herself. He knew, then, she would not last long in this hellhole. He was sick at his stomach, more from what he had seen then the smell. They were sitting on a filthy stone slab. There was dried blood and writing all over the stone walls . Walls that had black rings of iron and chains from them to match the ones on the stone ceiling.

Merena left Sister Authie and came to the bars. "You are still here?" she quietly asked. He hung his head and spoke in a low voice, "For a time, I can see what goes on here. I will wait until I can talk to De Caux". She just laughed bitterly to hear the tall knight talk this way," You still do not understand, do you? I will die here. I will be tortured in every way possible until I confess to what they want to hear, and then they will burn me in the public square!" He looked up, "But if you confess, if you take an oath DeCaux may be lenient."

Really?", she finally let the tears come, "How little you have seen what they do. What about these other people? Does this look like leniency? Look at the shape they are in after countless months of starvation and torture, they confessed months ago! And to what? and who did they have to name? Look on the street when you leave. You will see yellow crosses on clothing front and back. We know all about this. They will be the ones that confessed in public for everyone to see and abuse. They can be dragged back anytime,any year, to go through it all again. And no one can stop the inquisitors."

She went back to sit with Sister Authie. "You have done your job, you have brought me here to die with the rest. You might as well leave, unless you wish to stay and see it.." There was nothing he could say, she was right. He realized he could do nothing, he had done his job. But he had not counted on these people being human beings, not the devils DeCaux thought them to be. He had not

counted on liking them, liking her; feeling helpless himself. Knights
do not feel helpless. "I am staying, DeCaux will return on the
morrow. We will see what he has to say. If anyone tries to harm
either of you scream as loud as you can. I am only in the outer
room." He turned and walked away, unable to say anything else..

CHAPTER 18

1254 A.D. Carcassonne, France, Le Mur Prison

Old Simon hobbled into the prison as quick as his sticks
would push him along. He looked for someone to talk to when he
saw the knight sitting on a stone bench. "You were with the
inquisitor who arrested the two women, were you not?", he asked
breathlessly. " Aye. I was", said Sir David, "and you were with the
women, a priest, with the women who were arrested as rebels of the
Church."

Father Simon sat down on the bench ,along side him, and the
knight took his sticks and stood them against the wall. "I used to be a
priest, now I am a monk. Where are the women?" The knight told
him what had

happened so far. " You are to be blessed son, for what you have done in staying here. I have been so worried. I came to do what I could but I do not know what. My only idea is to say that I am their confessor, their priest, to show their innocence. I must. Have they confessed to anything?"

The knight studied the old man's face. "They have not , but they will before tomorrow, I have no doubt of it. I hear your accent, you may speak English with me, It might be better here anyway. I doubt anyone in this place knows the language."

Simon nodded, "As you wish, and it will do better to tell you all I have to say." Mcdowell continued, "Are they innocent?", he asked, point blank, "and how is it you are here?" Simon just looked at him, "I might ask you the same question. Let me find the jailer first, I must talk to him. If you still want to know their story I will tell you, it is a long one."

The Knight nodded. "I do not think you will get very far with the jailer. He is as brutal as they come. He may allow you to see them but he will not listen to you, or care what you have to say. I think if I had not threatened, and stayed, they would have already have been harmed." Father Simon nodded, "He is in the next room? He cannot refuse them a priest, a confessor, no matter what."

He grabbed his sticks and hobbled to the open room he saw. The big guards stopped him but he demanded to see the jailer. The jailer looked up, surprised to see the old man. He was obviously with the Church but anyone who needed a confessor would not be in this area of the prison.

He motioned for the guards to let him through. He looked the old man over, from his tonsure that was almost totally bald to the cross hanging under his beard and around his neck, and his monks robe and sticks. Simon wasted no formalities." I want to see the prisoners brought in this morning, They are allowed to see a confessor under law, and Church law." The jailer did not miss his accent. "You are the priest of that village?"

"Father Simon knew a lie would come back easily. "No, but I am a priest and they are my friends." The jailer smiled. "You are friends with these rebel Cathar's then?" he said ,intending to implicate Simon. "Is there any proof of them being Cathar's?" countered Simon, "If not then you must allow me to see them. I say they are innocent. They need the comfort of the Church until this mistake is discovered."

The jailer smirked, knowing DeCaux's record with guilt or innocence. "You may as well see them tonight as their innocence or guilt will be determined tomorrow when 'His Grace' returns. You may not wish to be here if they are guilty, but I see you would not get far if they are. You got five minutes,no doubt your last with them."

He pointed to the guards to take them to the last cell. The old man kept up as well as he could for his time was passing. The women were huddled in the corner . Sister Authie looked as if she were in a trance, staring at nothing. He saw Merena holding her face with a bloody bruise forming on the cheek. "I got here as soon as I could with God helping," he said breathlessly.

She hurried to the bars. "You will endanger yourself", she said ,almost whispering, "You must not tell them you were with us all!" He patted her hand, " I have not, I have said I was a friend", he lowered his voice, "had I claimed to be your priest that would have come back to haunt us. I do not know what you want to say for your innocence but we must think of something. They will soon know you are not of that village, then what?"

She shook her head. "Then nothing, I think the only thing to say is that we were just beggars walking from village to village when we saw you, and helped you. Otherwise, they will find the others." Father Simon nodded, "I suppose that is best, but this inquisitor is very determined. I hope it may be enough."

" It will not be", she said, Sister Authie knows it, and I know it. It would be best for you if you leave here as soon as possible. You have put yourself in great danger today." He smiled at her, "You put yourself in great danger for me, and this is what it has brought you. Had you not taken me to the river, you would not be here."

She shook her head, "It was always just a matter of time, now we must hope the others have longer." Father Simon tried to think of something positive, "What of the knight out there? Is he trying to help in some way? He comes from close to my home, you know. I think we may have a friend in him." Merena just shrugged. "What can he do? For all I know he will try to discover information and testify here. He did help me this morning and for that I am grateful."

"What happened this morning?' he asked her but did not get

an answer. The guards took Simon by the arms and pushed him down the hall as he hobbled the best he could. "I will come back!" he called to her. "God will protect you!"

When he came to the outer chamber he saw a boy handing a large portion of bread and cheese to the knight , and a flagon of good wine. It was in a basket he left with him. "Here, sit and have a meal with me, said the knight, "If you can stand to eat with that smell. As you see I have sent for plenty. We shall eat, and drink, and all left will be given to the ladies."

The old man was grateful as he had not eaten since the day before, except for a sliver of bread. "But you do not think they will allow it do you? I have seen how they feed here." McDowell, spoke between bites of cheese. "I think this jailer and I have a small understanding, but we will not -once DeCaux comes. He cannot have any influence over me, but neither have I any power over him once he arrives. The women will eat today but tomorrow will be another matter. In the meantime,Father, we have a long night to sit here, tell me your story".

CHAPTER 19

1254 A.D. Carcassonne, France, Le Mur Prison

Sir David McDowell stood to stretch his six foot frame after the long night of sitting on stone and listening to a fantastic tale. The dawn was just breaking ,but the night had not stopped the cries of pain from the next room and beyond. It had ,also, not stopped the smell of fear and humanity.

"What you have told me is almost impossible to believe, especially this story of a bloodline, it's blasphemous in the Church's eyes if true" he said to the old man, "yet there are elements of truth in it, like what happened to you over time, your story of your time in England, sore knees, and aches and pains, as you say."

"It is all true, Sir David, whether you chose to believe it or not. These people may be about to execute the last known descendant of Mary Magdalene," he whispered," but they will never believe it. Not that it would make any difference, the Church has been afraid of the truth of her, that it would make itself known for many centuries. That is why they have remained hidden. They are a threat. ""Too many questions would have to be answered, too many church beliefs would suffer.

They will never allow it." McDowell shook his head, "It's unthinkable, if true it explains the Cathar's and other gnostic thinking. It explains why they have been hunted and executed. But it goes against everything I know. I thought my brethren were sympathetic because we our aim and duty is to protect the people, not kill them. "

But he went on as he paced to get his blood flowing. "You know, as a boy, I heard of this Jongleur. It was one of the stories my tutor entertained my brothers and I with as small boys. He said he died with the other rebels, if he ever even was real. No one ever heard of him again.."

Father Simon nodded, "I burned the only evidence of his survival from Montsegur. The Church knew it was sent to me, they wanted it to destroy all knowledge of Jongleur, and what he knew. I

could not let that happen. He was as much my son as a real son.
Thousands of people know he existed and what he did, but they are
all 'rebels' as you call them."

" I call them Godly people who did not buy into untruths that
the Church needed to make it powerful and rich. I cannot expect you
to understand this. How difficult do you think it was for me, a priest
teaching new priests, to understand and accept? To even say it now?
After they killed Jongleur I made his mission, my mission. To find his
bloodline and to see it continue. I think he knew long before that he
would never survive to father a 'first daughter' to continue the line-or
even a first son."

" He knew many things before they happened. I have seen that
in Merena too. Right now, she knows what is to happen. She is a very
brave girl whose biggest concern, now, is for the others who remain
on that mountain. Even if they remain hidden they will not survive
long without her."

Sir David sat down with his head in his hands. "Aye father,
there's nothing that can be done. Even if we wanted to help, the
brethren and the Church would be at war over this. They are
dependent upon each other in this world"

Father Simon, patted his shoulder, "I know it, I'm not asking
you to endanger yourself them, or interfere . Indeed, I do not see what
can be done either. But these are wonderful, Godly, people, none of
them deserve to die. As for Merena, she is the future of the bloodline
and the gifts they carry, or she is the end of it for all I know."

McDowell looked at him, "Aye , what have we humans done to each other. Battle is bad enough, it is our nature as men and protectors, but this...this torture of people that has gone on because they do not fall under the thumb of the Church. It is a sin, no, it is more than that if what you tell me is true. It is deliberate cruelty and tyranny , centuries of lies and hiding the truth!" He was on his feet again. " You cannot talk to DeCaux, he will arrest you too. We need to get you out of here and I can help with that."

Father Simon gave him a weak smile. "Son, I told you she saved my life, it is not likely I would leave if I could help save hers. Mine is close to the end but hers is just beginning."

Just then, Bernard DeCaux walked into the prison with an entourage of twenty Temple knights. As he took off his long, blood colored cape he noticed the knight, and the monk he had sent on his way. He considered them. ' They have no business here now, 'but he would find out why they remained. It must have to do with the two prisoners he would begin to interrogate. That would be discontinued immediately. He would tolerate no interference when it came to these rebels.'

Father Simon hobbled after him into the cell room. DeCaux had taken a white lace handkerchief from the pocket of his robe and held it to his nose. "I wish to speak to Your Grace, about the two prisoners you sent here."

The jailer stood with his arms folded and smiled at DeCaux as he questioned Simon. "You are the monk that was with them, where is your diocese?" Simon answered. " I come from Britain, on

my way to a pilgrimage, if I can get there. The women were going to

the village to beg when they saw me fall and bandaged my foot. It is a

sprained ankle , I am afraid it is worse now, from the fall . I may need

to stay in this area until it heals." he added. " This is a widow and her

daughter, Your Grace, they are not who you seek. I got a ride here

from a farmer so I can speak for them. I only got to talk with them for

five minutes, but I know they are innocent . If you will but talk with

them you will see I am right."

DeCaux nodded his head, " If you are right I will see, but I

can tell you they are not innocent. I have years of files in my office. I

have just come from there, and I am assured they have the name of

other rebel Cathar's whom I have had burned. They will be

interrogated like any other prisoner and they will suffer other

penalties if they do no provide names of any who remain, and there

must be those who remain...these women could not survive alone.",

his voice rose excitedly. " I have no signed Edict from these women.

We shall see what they have to say".

The young knight had been leaning on the door entrance to

give his seat to other knights waiting on DeCaux. He came forward.

"I, too, am concerned about these women. I saw no evidence of them

being rebels in the two days they were with me, and Sir Reginald.

They are poor, without husband or father."

The inquisitor smiled at McDowell, knowingly, "Yes, she is

very pretty, is she not? Though I am surprised at you as a Templar.

Does your Preceptory in Scots land not hold to chastity, young man?
Remember, Satan has sent woman to tempt men into sin. Perhaps you
have forgotten your prayers today?"

Sir David felt his face reddening with anger. Other knights
looked on as he raised his voice in answer. "Your grace, I have
already seen how your prison deals with the people you send to them,
guilty or innocent. Your jailer left the imprint of his ring on the face
of one, and the other was frightened into hysteria. The women in
other cells tell another story. Insulting me will not alter that. I think
the pope would not appreciate his sheep being treated so cruelly if he
knew".

"You Templar knights ", Decaux spit out at him, " so self
righteous, so sure of yourselves, I guess you are not aware the pope
is unwell, his business right now is dying. And he will die with one
thought , that is to rid the world of these evil rebels. This I will do
with every one I find. In fact, I plan on sending your brethren back to
that mountain to look for others. They hold to the caves and where
there were two, there are more, just like rats."

He took his fur lined gloves off and waved them at the knight
to dismiss him. " You can take your opinion back to Scots land with
you, I have no need of a guard who would talk to me in such a
manner. I do what I wish here, or does my reputation not follow me
with the Temple?" The knights standing around waiting were none
too happy with DeCaux's remarks . They said nothing but some of
them looked grim.

DeCaux turned his back on the young knight, and Father
Simon started moving toward the jailer, but McDowell walked up to
him again, "Your Grace, I will need to make a report to the Templar
Preceptory here, and in Scotland. I shall remain here until my
prisoners have been released, or charged." He looked DeCaux in the
eye. He felt the blaze of the inquisitor glare,then turned his back and
strode down the cell block.

The other knights ,listening ,either shook their heads at him,
or smiled at him. DeCaux came to the door. "All of you , but for two,
join the other guards at the Preceptory. I will send a message if I am
to be kept here with business.

Two knights flanked the entrance door as the others filed out.
DeCaux and the jailer watched as Mcdowell stopped at the end cell.
He had a remaining hunk of cheese in one hand and half a small loaf
of bread in the other. DeCaux motioned to his two henchmen to stand
down there and listen. The knight saw that the women had been given
no place to relieve themselves during the night but the cell floor.

They would have to eat his small offering of food amid the
flies, bugs and other vermin in the cell. Sister Authie was still silent,
and staring, in some other world. Merena came to the door when she
saw him. She was wringing her hands in anxiety. " I could hear what
you said. You must take Father Simon away, and not get involved
yourself. You cannot help and will only be in danger, both of you."

He sighed." It is too late not to be involved in this. Father
Simon has told me all about you, and the others. I know who you are.
"Most young ladies facing what you are would be crying for help, why
are you so different?"

She leaned into the bars and almost whispered " Listen to
me, I have lost everyone but this family of women I protect. It is
useless to fight these men. Two months ago, before I met Father
Simon, I might have, now I know more after listening to Simon. They
will use any means to find out what I know, and now will know who
I am through torture. Since I learned of my family I know who hunts
me. I can see how futile it would be to fight them any longer . I am
tired of the work it takes to survive.. If you wish to help me, let it be
to protect the others on the mountain before they become victims. I
have no idea how you could do it but please try to help them. You can
do nothing here."

He was quiet, thinking for a moment, " But you can do
something, you can sign his Edict. You can wear the yellow cross if
you have to, you can say what he wants you to say, and live." She
slowly shook her head and walked back to Sister Authie.

She thought of all the others who died no matter what they
said or did. "Never", she said to him. "Time is short, if your heart
tells you this is not right, help the others however you can. The
children...they will even kill them. I wish to take the consolamentum.
If Father Simon does not know it he can give me the last rites, though
if Sister Authie ever speaks again she could do it. It is over for me".

CHAPTER 21

1254, Toulouse, France. The Villa

Word has come that the King will be expelling all Jews
from France, one way or another. He has come back after losing the
battle in Egypt. The Crusade has failed. In the meantime, the
Mongols have enslaved two hundred thousand people in Korea, and
taken them away.

The Church has declared a new belief for all Christians,
called Purgatory. It is a place, they say, between Heaven and Hell.
Unless people get intercession from the priests in their confessions
that is where they will end up when they die, perhaps in eternal
Limbo. Of course those given a clean slate from sin will not have to
endure this question the rest of their lives. That includes those who
murder men , women, and children . This is commanded by the pope
and inquisitors. All Catholic's are required to accept it under Church,
or any other Law. The confessionals must have lines of sinners,
terrified of a place of uncertainty after they die, with no guarantee of
the Paradise they were trying to earn. The saints in heaven now must
now be working even harder to intercede.

Church tithes have doubled I imagine , and the coffers will be
flowing down the line. of clergy. If that sounds bitter of me think of
it. You, where ever and whenever you are, must know how the
average man and woman struggle to stay alive. The large families
have many rumbling stomachs to fill. They go to bed hungry . As an
orphan I

remember, even at my age, how painful hunger was, how a scrap thrown to a dog made a difference on whether I ate that day, if I was quick enough to take it away from the dog. The Order found me just in time and must have seen more than hunger for food in me. I have to be strong enough to erase the pictures of children from my mind. How does one keep going? Like the common people, if I thought that all this lifetime of suffering would just lead to more suffering in this Purgatory ,instead of a seat in the paradise of Heaven, I would make my confession ;then hope I died that very day!

Meanwhile, there is gossip from clergy who come in here, that the Pope, Innocent IV, lays in his palace in Lyons, not far from death. It is no secret that he has groomed his nephew, Rinaldo Di Jennes, to take his place. He has given him every important position he can in order they he may gain the position. He was first a deacon, and then a Cardinal. Now he is the head of the Cardinals.

It is said he will take the name Alexander IV and will continue fighting Frederick the Great's son as he did the father. Frederick the Great was excommunicated twice before he died in 1250, as were other leaders of countries, and Rinaldo has promised to excommunicate Frederick's son as well. There is private communication that indicates he will escalate the Inquisition, and the Bull of torture.

This will make the inquisitors very happy indeed. In fact, Bernard DeCaux has not ever let that be a hindrance . I have had the report included here of trouble in Carcassonne that seems to be including a sentinel. I have no way to contact him but he must think twice before interfering, Although a tragedy may occur of unthinkable proportions , the Order must not be known or brought to light. I am sure they have cautioned him, but I am torn; wanting him to take action as well, though it be forbidden.

We continue to watch the family we monitor, preserving their identity , and truth for history. Pray that DeCaux continues to Italy where the Cardinals gather to await for the Pope's death. The business of the Papacy will keep the inquisitor busy until there is an outcome. There may be a way ,yet, he can influence the voting although the nephew awaits the mitre and the trappings , himself ,as new pope.

CHAPTER 22

1254 A.D. Carcassonne, France. Le Mur prison

The jailer was not on the cell block as McDowell left the room. DeCaux was in the outer room sending messages with another of the prison guards. Father Simon had fallen asleep on a bench in the corner while McDowell returned and took a seat next to him.

DeCaux sent the guard on his way, and then saw the knight sitting there.   " I will be questioning your two prisoners all afternoon so there is no point in your staying here. It is a lengthy process that must be done today as my guards and I must take our leave. I am already two days delayed from this important trip.""By the way, neither of you will be allowed to see the prisoners again until I finish, as the law states. I have just sent messages to the pope and his assistant with claims that you are making my duty difficult, in case you intend to cause further problems here. Also, the Temple Preceptory has just been sent a message for fifty of the knights to leave ahead of me as soon as they can get ready. They are to comb the area ,where we found these women ,for more Cathar's."

The old man had awoke with DeCaux's speech and got to his feet. " DeCaux smiled a fake smile at him. " Oh, and ..Father Simon is it? I have just sent a message to the Archbishop of Canterbury to

let him know you are here, and well. He surely will be pleased to hear
you are doing the pope's bidding."

The men said nothing until DeCaux left the room then sat
down to discuss what to do next. "We cannot push to see her now,
Father." Sir McDowell gathered his cape and helmet from the bench.
" You come to the Preceptory with me . We will have a good meal
and you can rest in a bed. I must contact Master LeBlanc and make a
report. I am at a loss to do anything else until we hear the charges, I
have seen them, already ,this morning. Sister Authie is no better,far
from it, and Merena says there will be no confession, and no Edict."

Father Simon nodded, "I thought as much. Her people will
not utter, or take an oath, and if she did she would be confessing by
doing it. That is a death warrant, no matter what the Church says. In
fact it is worse than death. They could keep her in here for years if he
wants. If she is let go they can call haul her in any year to reexamine
claiming it is a continuation of the investigation. She is in a losing
battle."

McDowell wrestled with his thoughts, "So, that is why she
told me she wants you to give her last rights, or something called a
consolamentum." The old man sighed. "Merena is preparing to die.
The consolamentum is a kind of final baptism ceremony with water, a
prayer commending the spirit, and a laying on of hands by a bishop or
parfaite of their faith. I could do it, as well as the last rites. It would
certainly be against my own church vows to do such a thing but they
are basically the same ceremony" .

"You have lived against the Church tenets since you have
been with them, have you not?" "Oh, much longer than that," he said.
"I have been meeting with the rebels I could find for many years,
looking for Merena. I became an enemy of the Church the moment I
burned Jongleur's manuscript about the bloodline descendants. Since
then I am no longer qualified to hear confessions, give communion or
any other priestly function. That is why I stepped back and became a
simple monk. When DeCaux receives a message back from the
archbishop he will know exactly who I am, and he will know exactly
who Merena is. And I will be sought for punishment as well."

        "We have to get you out of here, then. I did not tell you that
she requested that I help the other women instead of her." Father
Simon grabbed his crutches, " This will all reach a climax today. I
will go with you, but I will return and do as she wishes. We will know
the truth of his interrogation by then. Prepare yourself for the kinds
methods they may use, Sir David.   They must give her a hearing first,
surely DeCaux cannot start his punishment before that." Father Simon
pressed the knight's arm, " There is no real law for these people, even
Temple knights might be ordered to kill them without question. Ask
your brethren about Montsegur, about Albi, about the twenty
thousand put to the sword at Beziers. DeCaux knows what she is,
make no mistake, today he will use persuasions to find out who she
is."

        Sir McDowell looked grim. " I do not plan on being gone
long, just long enough to talk to Brother Montague, make a report to

Master Leblanc, and collect my travel expenses. We will get you settled, and I will call for you later this afternoon. The old man nodded, glad to have somewhere to rest..

" David" he cautioned, "I would not count on Sir Reginald too much even if he is from home, he has been a Templar many years, I imagine. He knows that in spite of the Temple 's feelings about the wrongness of killing their own people, ultimately , even they must comply with the wishes of the pope, and his clergy. They manage to walk a careful line which allows the knights of the Temple to have great freedoms." McDowell laughed bitterly. "Aye, yet freedom seems to be what it is all about. I am a Scotsman, we have shed much blood for freedom. I am also a Temple knight, my brethren have shed blood by the hundreds in the crusade, and to protect Christians, to allow them to worship in the land where it began.. How much blood will Merena's people have to shed for freedom? Who will fight for them?"

CHAPTER 23

1254 A.D. Carcassonne,France, Le Mur Prison

The three men left the Preceptory at three of the clock that afternoon. Simon had eaten and rested. Sir McDowell had gained the support of Brother Montague to go back with him to 'The Wall' , Le

Mur prison. The Master of the Temple had counseled McDowell to
'be careful and sure of the rightness of any of his actions'. " Brother
David, " he told him, " DeCaux creates chaos when it serves his
purpose. Keep your record clean."

It was good advice, but too late for him now, and Father
Simon too. They had already made an enemy. Before they had gone a
block back to the prison a messenger was sent running by the Master
to tell them DeCaux had left early that afternoon with the entire
Templar guard, proceeding again to Spain and then Italy.

They had to hurry, but before they got further they saw a
small crowd had formed in the village square. They saw people
throwing rocks at something. ',Do we check it out or get to the
prison' ?, they glanced at each other in question. As soon as they saw
the smoke rise the decision was made.

They ran, with Simon limping behind as fast as he could.
McDowell had a terrible feeling. He should not have left the prison
after all. As they got closer they could see a person was standing,tied
to the stake in the village square. A bonfire had just been lit and
flared into five foot flames. One piercing scream shattered the air as
they got closer, and then silence except for the din of the crowd
watching. The men held their breath as they got close enough to see
the persons face before the flames engulfed them... But it was too late
for the woman being consumed in the flames. It was Sister Authie.

Father Simon began heaving with great sobs. He had to be held up
by the knights. But McDowell could not stop for him. "Meet me
there!" he called back to Brother Reginald. "Be ready for anything!"
he yelled. He had his sword drawn as he entered the prison. One
guard stood at the entrance to the cell block. McDowell's eyes were
steel as he surprised the guard at the outer door.

"You can move or you can die!" he told him. The guard had a club
the size of a table leg, and a dagger. He advanced and the knight
knocked the club out of his hand with one swing. The guard lunged at
him with the knife catching him on the shoulder, the point barely
going through the tight chain mail. The knight's sword put a gash in
his neck that severed his artery. He dropped.

By that time the Jailer had heard the noise and was coming out of
a cell. McDowell pointed the sword at him, " Back up, get back in
that cell if you want to live". The jailer stood there but his eyes
showed fear. The guards at the back of the cell block had seen all,
and were coming.

"Now!," McDowell ordered, and surged forward. The jailer
stepped back as the knight slammed the bars in his face and turned the
key. The two guards were upon him and had him against the wall.
One had a knife and the other a sword. The knife put a gash in
McDowell's forearm where the chain mail stopped, but the other
guard lost his sword with one swing of the knight's sword crashing
against guards short sword.

In the fray McDowell lurched from the wall swinging as he

went. It caught the guard, without the sword ,in the side and spilled his
organs on the stone floor .The man stood in shock while the other
guard grabbed the sword off the floor. But he was an instant too late
as McDowell's sword suck deep in his chest. Blood covered the floor.
The jailer was too scared to call for anyone, the knight had fought like
a caged animal. "Are these all the keys ?" he demanded as the jailer
pointed to a drawer in the desk and McDowell got the other ring. "Get
on your knees and say your prayers", he told the jailer. "You may , or
you may not live, it depends on what I find in that cell." Just then he
heard a noise and spun around. Sir Reginald had just entered with
Father Simon behind him. They looked at the bodies and the
bloodbath in both rooms.

"Bolt that door, Brother Montague, McDowell told him, "I
do not want to kill anyone else unless I have to. Go down to the other
door at the end of the cell block. and stand guard for me.."

McDowell proceeded down there ahead of Montague. He got
to Merena's cell holding his breath. "Oh God! Come and help me,
Reginald!" Merena was hanging from the ceiling about six feet off
the floor. She was suspended, bare to her waist, hanging from thick
iron rings by her wrists, swinging slowly to and fro. Her head was limp
against her naked chest. "She's alive, if just barely.", he called to
Father Simon, who was making his way down the cell block.

There was dead silence in the cell block from the people who
had heard and seen all the killing. Blood covered the floors and walls.
McDowell tried the smaller keys on the ring until he found one that
opened the hanging rings. She was unconscious and badly bruised on

her arms and back. One eye had blackened from the blow of the ring the jailer had given her the day before. They lowered her to the stone bench. McDowell ripped off the lower third of the undershift he saw under the long skirt which remained from her dress. He used his dagger in his boot to cut a piece off, wrapped the remainder around her chest and tied it.

"Get some water on this, and some water for her to drink. Simon limped in. " God Almighty! What have they done to her?!" he asked . Her eyelids flickered but did not open. Montague was back with the wet cloth, and water. McDowell washed her face and neck with the cold water, and she slowly gained consciousness.

" Oh! Thank God you have come! They took Sister Authie!," she cried out, "Hurry! You must help her!" Father Simon patted her hands and rubbed them. "Calm down, we have to get you out of here quickly. Do you think you can walk?", Sir McDowell quizzed her.

"Yes, I think so, but Sister Authie!' "What did they use on you?' he continued to quiz her as he wrapped his white cape around her. Her arms flopped until he tucked them in, she seemed to have no use of them. "You have been hanging here all night! " he said as he stood in the puddle of her urine beneath where she had hung.

"The guards carry clubs", she said in a low, breathless voice, "The inquisitor would leave the room and tell them to use them on my arms and back. I guess I passed out . They hung me up first, my arms got numb and then I felt like I could not breathe. I think they would not have stopped but he told them he had to leave. He said to keep me alive until he returned but it would be at least a month,....I am so glad you have come!" Her lipped quivered with the effort not to cry.

He helped her to stand but her legs would not hold her so he scooped her up. "Got any ideas where we can take her?" he asked Montague. "Well, it cannot be the Preceptory, " said the other, "or the church, they could not cross DeCaux. Maybe someone's house?"

Just then two more guards came out the door next to the end cell they were in. Sir Montague's reflexes did not fail him. He shoved the open cell door into the first guards face, knocking him out. The second guard tripped over the first, and lunged at the knight with a long knife. Montague parried, then knocked it from his hand , his sword slicing the man's two fingers off.

The guard held his hand ,screaming... Montague put his sword point on the guard's chest and backed him into the second cell block. He slammed the door, between them, and bolted it, jamming the guard's long knife under the wooden bar for good measure.

McDowell was already half way down the cell block with Merena. Sir Reginald passed Father Simon and unbolted the door to the outer chamber. McDowell threw him the key ring he had slipped over his belt. "Quick, unlock all those other cell doors. Tell those boys to send for someone to help those who cannot walk get out of here. I'll meet you at the stables". He passed Father Simon heading outside. He was about to tell him they had to find somewhere quick. Suddenly, a wagon full of hay pulled up in front of the prison, "Get in!" the driver called to them . Father Simon looked at a shocked McDowell. "It is good!" said the monk, "he is a friend!".

. "You!", the knight yelled to the stable boys, " get inside and tell the other knight I said to meet us at the edge of town with our horses. Tell him to give you a coin for your silence! You would not inform on knights ,I think?" The boys eyes were huge as they shook their head at the great adventure he saw unfolding.

Sir McDowell gently laid Merena in the hay and covered her completely, making room for her to breathe. He lifted the frail Simon up to the wagon seat with no trouble and jumped up himself. "Go!," he said. The guard on the wall saw nothing amiss with the wagon that went out the entrance, except that a monk and a knight were riding with a farmer. Two miles outside Carcasonne the fast moving team had pulled behind a grove of trees and bushes to wait for Sir Reginald.

"Thank you!", Sir McDowell said to the driver, "whoever you are, now what?" Father Simon quickly told him this was the driver who had brought him all the way from the mountain; that he had been going to Carcasonne to get his brother. "Where is your brother now, anyway?" Simon said to him." The driver hesitated, "Oh , he dragged me away from the farm and then said he had decided to stay at the monastery until his living started.. I do not blame him either, he is no farmer and he cannot cook, he'd just be in the way."

The knight got off the wagon to check on Merena who was crying softly. "You must be in much pain." the knight said gently. "That is not it," she said, "we have gone off and left Sister Authie with those killers." He tried to be easy with her. "We were not in time. DeCaux had them burn her late this afternoon. I am sure he did it to weaken you to confess, to break you."

Her eyes were heavy with tears as she shook with grief, " Oh no, my poor friend! It would have if I had known, as it was I passed out . I would never have lasted. He told them to put me on the rack if the clubs did not work. Now, I hate to think what they did to Sister Authie.."

She tried to turn away but her body was too beat up to move. There was nowhere to touch her that was not bruised ,from the night before ,and this morning. He tried to comfort the crying girl. "She was out of her mind with fear, I do not think she suffered long." he offered. Just then Simon spotted Sir Montague coming, and McDowell waved him to where they were.

" You know where you are going?" said Montague, reining in both horses. "They are on their way to look for the others on the Mountain, " said Sir McDowell, " I was hoping you might come with us to help." Merena called softly from the wagon, "Oh please do, you have seen what will happen to them, he will kill them all!" "All who"?, he puffed.

"He does not know yet", said McDowell, "Reginald, Merena has kept twenty women and two children alive for eight years on that mountain. They are the rebels, the Cathar's. Sister Authie was one of them." Father Simon wiped a tear running down his old face. "They all took care of me, Sister Authie carved this beautiful walking stick

for me. Believe me, they were nearer to God on his mountain than
DeCaux could ever hope to be."

Sir Reginald looked at McDowell . He was angry at what he
had seen and it showed on his weather beaten face.. "I am a Templar,
we do not hold with barbarians like these, and the abuse of women,
count me in!." Sir David shook his hand, "That is just what I
thought!"

Montague had just noticed the man on the wagon. "Who's
the driver?" "A friend!", yelled Father Simon and McDowell at the
same time. "Let 's go!"

CHAPTER 24

1254 A.D. Back to Bugarag mountain

They stopped for the night as darkness fell. The wagon
would not climb those steep hills in the dark. There was no food but
the round loaf of expensive wheat bread the driver said he was taking
home. He split it between all of them.

Some of the hay made the ground a little less hard for the
knights and the driver, while Merena, and Father Simon used the
remainder in the wagon. As McDowell laid down, Simon noticed the
cut on his arm with a piece of cloth tied around it. "Do not worry,"
Simon told

him, "Merena will fix that up for you.!" Sir Montague asked the other knight, under his breath, "Have any idea how we will rescue these women or what we do with them afterwards?" McDowell shook his head. "No idea," he said, "we gotta get them first". They heard Simon snoring, and little noises told them Merena was crying, no doubt about her good friend Sister Authie. "Lucky thing you came by when you did," he said to the driver. "Yes, lucky", said the sleepy voice.

They started right before dawn. The white circle of a late June moon could still be seen as it gave up the night. Merena was able to sit up but it would be a few days before she would have use of her arms and bruised back. McDowell decided that nothing seemed broken in her arms. Of course he could not tell about the ribs, but she had just taken a severe beating. It was their first intention to scare her; convince her she would come to greater harm if she did not confess.. DeCaux had known it would not kill her. He wanted her alive and willing to talk when he returned, if she had lived through the rack and the lack of food and water .

Merena sunk down in the hay when horses passed. where they hid. " We have not much time." stated McDowell ". One of these horsemen no doubt carries a message to DeCaux. He will stop again if he is not into Spain yet. The wagon slows us but we need it for the women...You will let us have it for this rescue, will you not?". The driver nodded. "The less I know about this, the better", he added". I can have you drop me, and I will walk to my brother's farm. It is not far from the mountain, but it is well off the main path."

McDowell shook the hand that did not hold the reins," God must have sent you to us to do His work." The driver smiled, "I am sure it was something like that", he said. Merena said from inside wagon. "I have been thinking all night what we could do but it would mean we would have to keep this wagon, or get another one."

" Also, Sir McDowell, it would mean you ,and your friend. would have to help us even more. It is the only way I can see a chance for us to leave the area , and the country. There are too many of us not to be discovered ,and arrested. I do not know how I can ask more after all you have done. If it is too much, you must just tell me. Surely there must be some way."

"Tell me, then", said McDowell, "because I cannot think of one way to get them off that mountain. "I do not see how you can do anything, Merena, in your condition," sighed Simon", and I will be no help at all" Merena shifted herself again in the rocking wagon which agonized every bone and muscle in her body ."I will think of something", she offered.

Chapter 25

1254 A.D. Bugarag Mountain

They arrived in the afternoon. The driver pulled behind a
hillside. "This is where I leave you," he told them. "I will make some
excuse about the wagon to my father and brother." Sir Reginald
dismounted and reached inside his long Templar cape where two
small bags of coin rested, and handed one bag of coin to the driver.

"This should help you to find a reason," he told him. The driver mentally weighed the small bag. "I cannot take this, it is enough for two or three wagons" .

"I am glad" said Sir Reginald. " We are near Couiza, You should be able to buy a better wagon and horses to go home in, and have money left, without your help all would be lost for these women." Sir Mcdowell turned to him, " You need not give your money, I got you into this." But Sir Reginald shook the drivers hand . "Go on," he said. "I took a vow of chastity, so I will have no wife or children, and the Temple fills all other needs ,so what do I need it for?"

The driver smiled, and wished them luck finding the others. He headed down the dusty road amid thanks from all of them. Mcdowell took the reins while Sir Reginald tied the extra horse to the back of the wagon. The dust from other horses was spotted in the distance coming toward them so they lumped the hay up over Merena and proceeded on. The group of ten Templar knights came upon them and slowed to a stop. They had come from the mountain.

"What are you doing"? said the leader in the group, giving the sign. He recognized his fellow brethren traveling , but out of most of their armor. McDowell growled, "We were told to take this monk back to the village; he cannot ride with that foot. He's taking the wagon back to his monastery. They farm here in the country, you know. What about you, my Brothers? I thought you were guarding DeCaux to Spain and Italy." They reined the horses around the wagon.

"He's gone with the others, and not happy with us at all." said the lead knight. " We were sent to look for the rebels with him. He climbed as high as his horse would without throwing him, but he is not used to anything but the road. We circled the bottom, and he urged us to climb higher. We tried but we carry too much weight to get any higher. A couple of men tried to walk it, but too steep further up, so we thought we would come around to find an easier route."

" His Grace told us to send a message if any rebels were found, and, if not, go back to the Preceptory and get more help. I tell you he was in a mean state when none were found ,and when we didn't leave our armor and climb. "

"McDowell spoke up again. "We are headed back, too, after we drop the friar off. We can make another run up the mountain when we are done if you like. No need for help, I can get up there and take a look. " Sir Reginald nodded in agreement. "Sure , he's more fit than most of us. You men can go on back."

Two or three of the brethren discussed it together. "Yes", the knight in front said, "since you are here you may as well. You took the first ones back so you know what to do if you find more." The two knights nodded in agreement; they all gave the sign and rode on.

Sir Reginald looked grim when McDowell glanced back at him. He knew the one thing a Templar would never do is lie to his brethren. Above all that was a vow that could not be broken, one of the most important rules in the Code of Chivalry.

"You can go back too if you want," he told him, "you have

done enough. The Brothers would understand, they do not like this brutality any better than we do".

Sir Reginald had gotten to like the young knight as they traveled together from the Isle of Britain. And he saw the helplessness of the people they hunted. " I said I would stick with you, Brother. That is what we do, thick or thin. I have fought alongside many, but I think of only one whom I feel would have my back more than you, and he is dead. No, I will see this through. Carry on."

Merena had lain quiet until now. She sat up and looked both ways at the empty road. "I know what the two of you must have sacrificed for me, so far, and what I am asking you to do. I know my gratitude will never be enough, it is just that these women have suffered so much, lost so much, and you can make a difference in whether they live or die, like you just did for me."

" It seems to me you truly have kept a higher vow of your order than the one you just broke. I know God will hold you in his mercy, and bosom." McDowell looked at Sir Reginald and nodded toward Merena.. "This is who they hunt down and torture to death", he said, "let us get on our way, for the day grows short."

Merena pointed to a field through the trees, " Go that way, the field goes all the way to the bottom of the mountain. Then we must keep to the left and drive as high as the wagon can make it. This side cannot be seen as well and that is why our camp is there, very high up. You will have to hide the wagon behind trees; though if anyone does see. they may think it is a farmer." McDowell nodded, "We will have to hide the horses low, they will just drag us down."

They came to the mountain base on the west side and began ,
slowly, up the gentle incline until the wagon was leaning to the left.
"We cannot go much further or the wheels will collapse", he told
them. "Better find cover quick."

Merena pointed to a grove of pines. "Can you make it
there?" she asked. That would shelter the wagon, and be good grazing
for the horses as well." He dropped down a level to be closer; take
the strain off the wheels, and started back up again ,cutting to the
right this time. The wagon made it behind the trees, although they
would have to chock the wheels in back.

The horses were tied a few yards away. Sir Reginald looked
up to the expanse of the mountain still looming over them and began
taking off what remained of his armor and stacking it in the wagon.
"I hope we can get up there", he sighed to them. Merena got to her
knees, gingerly, and saw she was at such an angle in the wagon that
she would have to have help to get out. "I will have to take you the
way I know, this side is too tricky, too steep, unless you know how to
get up it." McDowell shook his head, "I do not see how you could
possibly make it, you can barely walk as it is."

She was standing and holding on to the side, "I will have to,
it would scare them to death to see you alone. Several of the women
are older and not in very good health anyway." Father Simon had been
silent all this time letting them figure out how to get the wagon there.
He was holding on for dear life as the wagon angled down the steep

hill. "I am not going to be any help, you can take my stick, and the
cane Sister Authie made me."

" We will see what we can do," chimed in Sir Reginald. "We
can always come back for you with a litter. We just need to get up
there ourselves." The agreement was unspoken. Mcdowell came
around and lifted the waiting Merena to the ground. Her legs were
weak, but she stood looking toward the summit. He handed her the
sticks but he had decided to carry her if she hesitated at all. She
could not manage the sticks, it was obvious her arms were pretty
useless under his Templar cape.

She continued to look up. "What are you staring at?" he
asked. "I am looking at that misshaped rock near the top with a
square hole in the middle. That is our lookout and we usually have
someone there. It is not likely they could be seen from here anyway
but they might see us if one of you waved his arms it might let them
know a friend was coming." Both knights stood and waved
vigorously, but not long. They needed to conserve strength for the
climb.

Sir David had already figured out what he would do. He
stripped to a light woolen undershirt and gave his longer outer shirt
to Merena to wear., discarding the heavy surcoat. Then he took the
girdle that held his short sword, and canteen; strapped Merena on his
back with it, in spite of her light protest. She had to carefully fold her
injured arms between her body and his back so they would not have to
dangle. "I do not see how you can climb with my weight too." He

laughed, " your weight is nothing to the weight we carry with armor and gear, and Sir Reginald will lead the way to stop any fall we take. We will be back for you Father Simon, yell if you see anyone approaching."

And they started up the most difficult area of the mountain. McDowell could feel the strain in his legs as he, step by step, navigated the steep hills. "Keep to the left", Merena said, "Kick those bushes out of the way", she told Sir Reginald, "they hide a path I have been using for eight years. Now go around that great rock until you see a plateau."

They made their way slowly with McDowell falling behind, and Sir Reginald forging ahead and dropping back to wait on them. They came to the first plateau and rested. Merena stood down to take her weight off. They looked down on the valley that had left behind, saw where the wagon looked well hidden.

Merena pointed to large rocks for them to sit on. "This is where I found Father Simon", she said pointing to a grove of trees, "I think he broke the ankle on one of these rocks. He was lucky his head did not hit it. And if it had been anywhere else away from this harder to climb area, I doubt I would have ever seen him." She pointed to the cliff above. "That is where he fell from."

The men looked at it, marveling how he survived at his age. " He must have been pretty cut up all over, and... you healed him?", noted Sir Reginald. "It had been a few days", she said, " his infections would have been too far gone had it been even a day longer. As it

was, he was a very sick man. I think it helped that he had a will of
iron to complete a mission, he says he has, and I have just humored
him to get him better."

Sir Reginald took a hard look at her as they rested. " I want
to tell you something, Miss. Sir McDowell told me enough about the
old man's story, and it got me thinking. " I knew of this Jongleur he
told about. I was in Venice with my Templar brethren when I was
younger, twelve-thirteen years ago. I served with the finest man I ever
knew, whose name was Sir Geoffrey of Somerset. We had just come
back from fighting in Jerusalem, and the Doge of Venice was putting
an entertainment on for the returning Templar's."

" That night a troubadour was part of the dinner
entertainment. His name was Jongleur, the storyteller . He was
tall, hair like yours ,and had a way with words. He was magical while
saying them. It was almost spellbinding. One story he told was about
a beautiful, sweet girl who was burned. I even remember her name
was Emmalanna..something like that. Imagine us sitting there, fighting
men who see blood on a daily basis. It brought tears to our eyes.
Grown men were unable to hold it back,that is powerful. She had
been burned in England." he continued, looking down the mountain at
the miles of country that could be seen from where they were. "That
stuck with me because that is my home, you know. He told other
amazing tales and offended the Doge. When the soldiers were told to
attack him he produced fire ,out of thin air, to ward them off. He
disappeared that night, and along with him so did my Brother in the

Temple, Sir Geoffrey. I heard , later, that Geoffrey died at

Montsegur, defending your people. So you see, I would not doubt a

thing Father Simon said about him."

There was absolute silence when he stopped talking. Finally,

McDowell looked at him, " So this is why you had no trouble agreeing

to help in Carcasonne?" "Partly, said the older knight, " Sir Geoffrey

knew much more about this family, I believe. If he helped this

Jongleur he had a very good reason, and that is good enough for me,

we better get going again".

"You can see we cannot go up where Father Simon fell," she

told them." We must go a roundabout way. Walk here; far to the left

and start climbing up where you see the steeper grassy slope. It will

take us up to the second plateau. Then we take another left and go

aways, the camp will be there, or the women will be in the caves. I

will call out to them when we reach the plateau."

And so they began even a harder assent , one using handholds

she showed them on each side when it was too steep to walk standing

up. The valley under them was beautiful and expansive. Sir

McDowell marveled at the many miles away he could see. 'What a

great hiding place to watch for an approaching army' he thought.

Finally they pulled themselves up to the second plateau and

sat there panting. "I think I can walk from here if you help me",

Merena said to McDowell. "My legs feel stronger. " He put his arm

around her waist as she stumbled along the rocky ground and then

stopped suddenly. "Sister Garnier!, she called, Sister Legasse!, it is
Merena, I have come!" There was silence. She stepped down a level
holding on to McDowell, and around to the left another few yards, to
a large flat area hidden by pines, and there were the lean-to's.

" Sister Garnier come out, I am with friends!" Slowly,
women came from everywhere, out of the lean-to's, behind the trees,
and down from the caves directly above them. Sister Garnier ran to
her , hugging her while they all stared at the men with her. The two
children hid behind one of the women. "Sisters!", she said to them, "I
have brought help, these are friends and they will help us all!"

"Come on, come! " said Sister Garnier, excitedly, to them all.
"Sit , rest ,and tell us all. We saw the men take you away. It was
horrible! Where is sister Authie? Where is Father Simon?" The men
sat on stumps there and looked around at all the women gathering
around Merena ,all trying to hug her. The men quietly took in the little
lean-to village behind granite ,and a few trees they had survived in all
these years. One of ladies ran to bring water to each of them in
wooden cups carved by Sister Authie, another ran to stir whatever
food they had been able to put in the large pot on the fire.

The children peeked at the giant men from behind one women,
as the others bustled around camp. Another, a few years older than
Merena, stared at the handsome knights until she was nudged by an
older woman, then she got busy sweeping camp with their makeshift
broom tied with wild grape vines. "Come and sit," Sister Garnier said
to all the women, "let us meet these good men and

listen to their story. I must know first, is Sister Authie in prison? Do they have Father Simon too?"

Merena pointed down the mountain, "You cannot see him from here but Father simon is waiting for us in a wagon. He is fine, except needing a good rest. He could not climb yet, of course." They all listened eagerly as Merena told the story of her ordeal and rescue; the knights , somewhat embarrassed, added the parts she did not know, prodded by Merena. They finally came to to part they dreaded but it had to be said. Merena bravely took the lead.

"When they came back to help me the gentlemen saw a crowd baying in front of a burning stake. The prison guards came and got Sister Authie that morning", she related dismally," and she was who they burned."

There was a gasp from the women, then tears for the gentle Sister Authie who had used her abilities to carve wood toys for the two children, implements to make their lives easier, and who always had an interesting tale or two about her old life. One of their own had died .

A few retired to their shared lean-to, others found work to do, and Sister Garnier said a prayer aloud with the remainder of the group gathered.   When it was done she turned to Merena, " So you have brought these brave knights to help us. What have you decided we are to do, I would think we have very little time. The inquisitor will take this very personally, they will be back for you and this time they will not be stopped."

Merena cupped her elbows so the weight was taken off her sore shoulders and arms. "We have brought the wagon, and I have a idea of what we can do. I just do not know where we can go even if we have the wagon to get there." "What is the idea?", broke in Sir David. Merena took a deep breath

. "It will take everyone to help.We would have to use our largest pot and, somehow, we would have to fill it with water. My stored elderberry would not be enough. More would have to be gotten. The walnuts would have to be cracked so I can add the hulls to the elderberry roots."

" We shall die each woman's dress and blanket black to create each a nun's habit .The black dress, the black blanket over the head, tied close to the neck with a wide band made from each underskirt, to cover the hair. Those who have no underskirt left can have a piece of someone elses. We would pose as a convent of nuns going somewhere, but where?"

"What about the two children"? someone said. "I have thought of that. They can be two orphans, which they certainly are,. We can be taking them to start an orphanage." Sister Garnier nodded, " A very wise idea, I do not know how you came up with it with everything you have been through, but it might work. Could the knights be taking these nuns somewhere?"

"That would not last long." chimed in Sir McDowell, "it will be a threat as long as you remain in France." Sir Reginald jumped up. "That's it!" he was excited. "I know where to take you, but it would

mean a long trip over the Catalonia trail. It is a well traveled route, a
mountain pass over the Pyrenees to sanctuary in Catalonia! La Ruter
Del Cister! the Cistercian route."

" They harbor many of your people who are able to escape
there, and there are three monasteries that I know of, and several
villages where you would be welcome." Merena was speechless, she
looked around at the women. "Why, that is perfect, it is not! ?" They
all nodded, excited for the possibility that they might find a decent
life somewhere

Sir Reginald scratched his head again, "You know, "he told
the group, "now that I think of it a better place might be Vielha. It is
in a large valley, very fertile, a very quiet and beautiful place with
mountains as far as you can see, very far indeed. There's lots of water
down from the mountains, for growing grapes and other crops....and
the people there are your folks, I am told, who have escaped there.
Naturally, they must all speak Occitan, or Catalan, much the same,
they tell me."

There was a surge of excitement from the women, most
whose lives had been in grape arbors and farmland. "The name is
Vielha?' someone asked. "Yes, it means valley, and it is in the Val
D'Aran, which also means valley in a valley." he told them. Sir
Reginald nodded,"It would mean a long, rough trip of over a hundred
miles, maybe two or three weeks of walking and riding" .

Sister Garnier looked at him wryly. " Sire, we have labored
on this desolate mountain for eight years, do you think we would

not be up to a long walk? I know our legs will be weak but they will get strong again." "That's right," enthused Merena, "some can ride and some walk and then take turns in the wagon. It is the answer to our prayers, Sir Reginald!" He nodded and went on with his plan.

"It is closer to a village called Berga, and one in Vallbona, but the biggest is Guimera. There they have a church, St. Mary's and it has a watchtower." Sister Garnier looked at Merena, "Is that where you would rather go, Memory keeper? Merena shook her head, "Maybe someday, but it sounds like the valley would be a wonderful life for everyone. I cannot wait to tell Father Simon . "Yes, we need to go get him," said McDowell .

Sir Reginald told the group, "I would not wait past tomorrow or the next day, the men may coming to look again. Besides that we must get you over those mountains and into the valley before winter. You must also have time to find or build homes and get crops started to feed yourselves."

The knights started down the mountain while the women looked to Merena and Sister Garnier for instructions. Merena's mind was racing , " First, we need water after we eat whatever you have in the pot. Then we need more elderberry and walnuts cracked . Someone get rocks to crack the nuts while the others can get water . Each of you can wear your blanket while your dresses are died in bunches. Then we can do blankets. We cannot take anything but foodstuffs and any other bedding. There will be no extra room in the wagon. "Sister Garnier nodded to her. "I will get them going, I think

with what you have been through you need to rest until we get it all
started." " You are forgetting one very important thing" Sir
McDowell said, lagging behind Sir Reginald down the mountain. He
called back to them,"You will have habits but no one will have a
cross." There was an audible gasp from the women. He walked back ,
resting one foot on a rock," Listen, you may not want to", he
continued, "but nobody is going to think you are nuns without them,
and everybody will be in danger."

Sister Garnier nodded, as he turned around and left again, "
He is right . And it is the price of our freedom, someone get branches-
get the straightest twigs and carve them. Who is the best with wood
since Sister Authie is not here?" Two women raised their hands . "
We will do it", one said," hardwood would be the
best-someone can make cords from the edges of the blankets to hang
them around the neck." They began to work on them immediately.
Merena rubbed her swollen arms, "And now there is so much to do,
the sooner we get away from the mountain the better we all will feel."

Chapter 26

1254, A.D. Bugarag mountain

The two knights made a litter to carry Simon up the
mountain until it was too steep, then took turns strapping him on
their backs. The women rushed to him as soon as they were in view;
happy to see him again, Sister LeGasse padded a stump with a flat
pillow stuffed with bedstraw for Simon to sit on. Another got him a
bowl of soup they had made from greens and chives they had found in
Merena's absence, and some of her herbs thrown it for flavor. It was
not much but it was all they had found.

McDowell decided he would go after some game to throw in
the pot,after he and Sir Reginald rested. This would be all they ate
today as the large pot was needed tonight to dye all the clothes and
blankets. They could dry rapidly in the wind on the mountain today,
and the pot would be scrubbed out for tomorrow's stew if he had
gotten enough game. That would be the last meal here on the
mountain.

That afternoon they had a filling,tasty rabbit stew thickened with roots and the last of the lentils. Then two of the women took the large pot to the water pool they used, washed it out and filled it to the brim with cold, fresh spring water. The two knights carried it back to the fire pit while others gathered elderberry, and cracked black walnuts with rocks.The nutmeats were stored to take with them and the hulls were thrown in the pot.

Merena supervised with both her arms resting in slings made from rags of old clothing.. Finally, the pot had a deep black color . The women took turns wearing their blankets while their long dresses were dyed and hung on trees to dry in the mountain air. As soon as they were dried they gave the blanket to the next person, and so on down the line ,while the pot boiled with more walnuts to keep the dye even. Soon all the dresses, and whatever underslips they had left, were done, the unbleached wool blankets were in the pot and ready to be dried all night. It was a hot ,end of June, night with no need for blankets. Those who had underslips left slept in them anyway, while the knights lay down in a pile of bedstraw Merena had shown them..

The next morning the soaking pot had to be scrubbed with salt to clean the dye residue before it sat up and stained the pot. The few pots they had were dear. With no money they would not have any others. They would not leave until later that afternoon. The blankets were not completely dry,plus they must gather what greens and herbs they could carry with them.

Merena showed them where to go and what to pick in the herb plants, especially what roots she would need for medicines.

These, most certainly, might be found where they were going, but perhaps not on the way. They could not take a chance with ailments, or accidents on the road.. Everyone had to be fit for travel.

They went down the mountain in twos or threes so as not to arouse suspicion should anyone be looking up to the mountain. The younger ones helped each other climb down the harder way, while the old ones took another route and cut across the second plateau to the wagon. Each woman carried a load with her of her blanket and what ever else she could carry.

The children were strapped to the backs of two younger women, while the two knights tied Merena and Simon on their backs to keep their hands free to descend. McDowell stopped at the wagon and decided to drive it further down the mountain another way so the wheels wouldn't snap off. They put Simon and Merena in first, and McDowell jumped on the wagon seat.

Sitting on the plank, he found the small bag of coins that Reginald had given the wagon owner! He threw it to Sir Montague. Sir Reginald shook his head and put it back in his inner pocket. "Wonder what they said when he walked in without that wagon? Ah well, we will have plenty use for this along the way, and maybe he knew that, but the horses too ."

They gathered, hidden behind trees at the bottom of Bugarag. They all took one last look at God's mountain that had sustained them all the years, then Merena and McDowell took one last look at them all in their black- dyed dresses, the bound crosses hanging round their necks, and the blankets covering their heads, secured at the neck. A white strip had been tied around the forehead and the blanket fell over the ears and was tied at the back of the neck. They looked at each other and nodded at the convincing group of poor sisters of the Church.

Sir Montague took the lead and Sir McDowell would ride with him as they were to be seen as the protectors of the group of nuns. Sister Garnier would drive the wagon until they were out of the village and into rough terrain. The others would walk until they got tired then take turns riding in the wagon. It would be a slow process with this many people.

Sir Montague said to them, "We will have to go through Montsegur and head to the Sampor pass, on the Templar trail. There are only a couple of ways to get over those mountains. .We will have to go south to Andorra then head west to the Val D'Aron. It is a long trip, and dangerous in many places. We will have to find a lower route for the wagon some of the way, and we may have to sell it and buy another when we get there. "

He mounted his horse, and had another thought," Ladies, you may find a place you'd like to settle before then. That is up to you, though I encourage you to go to that valley. You may see that you recognize your people as you go along, as many have fled there all along the border of the Pyrennies. It is a mingling of religions there, including Jews."

And so they took to the road and began the journey as nuns and pilgrims with their two , now armored ,escorts. No one looked back. They only made ten miles before nightfall, but it was good time

with the wagon and many older women. They found an open area
enclosed by trees well off the road. No one would see them .Hungry
bellies would have to wait until morning for food, where ever it
would come from. They camped off the road and sleep came early to
all.

Come morning, Sister Garnier drove the wagon the remaining
fifteen miles to Montsegur following Sir Montague's lead. They
veered around the village, It was the only wagon trail in the area ,
beaten down by years of traveling feet, wagons, and horses The
strange procession brought many stares but no one tried to bother
them.

On the road to Montsegur many legs unused to walking got
tired and had to rest in the wagon as there was no stopping . Merena
gave up her place a time or two in the day and a half, and the twenty-
five miles to Montsegur. The knights rode on each side so the wagon
would not have to drive over the horse droppings.

Soon they must find a way to bypass Montsegur. The knights
knew there would be too much suspicion and too many questions in
that town. Spirits were high in the group, though, especially the two
children. They were going to a new place where people would accept
them. They could hope for shelter and a different life off the
mountain. A life without fear. It kept them all going.

They would have to continue moving after Montsegur. The
knights would decide when to stop that night, and then they would
have to worry about food. They passed around the walnuts that had
been harvested to eat as they walked, to give them energy . The

knights were grim as they passed Montsegur, as were many of the
women. They urged no talking unless spoken to ;   that they ,
only,would answers any questions. They were to be as a
contemplative order going to Andorra to provide an orphanage,
bringing two children with them.

The tiny village below the high pog that was Montsegur was
still almost a ghost town ten years after the attack on the Cathar's
there. It was still in the memory of many of the women who may
even have been from there at one time, so the mood was quiet as
thoughts of those who died there were ever present. The village held
workers that were rebuilding and changing the destroyed fort. They
paid no attention to the troop going by. In fact there were many other
people joining the travelers on the old Roman road to the Somport
Pass ,leading over the mountain pass.

.The summer days were longer so they would be trudging as
many miles as possible. As they walked Sir Montague rode back to
one of the many vendors that made a living from the pilgrims going to
the various places of pilgrimage all the way to Santa Compostela,
,Spain to the pilgrimage of Saint James. It would take a lifetime of
savings for these devoted to go on their thousand mile pilgrimages,
and to stop at many shrines along the way.

Sir Reginald found a vendor to sell him a mule which he
loaded down with cheese, bread, and hides of milk. This they would
have when they stopped for the day. Tomorrow they would find game
and have a meal along the way. The food he got should last them a

few days, along with the game. Everyone ate a wedge of cheese as they walked and the children rested in the wagon and drank goats milk.

Their spirits lifted after the food that night, and they were able to go many more miles that next day before nightfall. They did not arouse much suspicion, as a group of nuns. In fact the pilgrims passing them gave them respect, nodding and smiling. Some crossing themselves, and bowing to them. Everyone was traveling in the months before winter when the mountains would not be passable until the next spring or summer.

Each day the walk continued early after dawn, as they passed pilgrims camped and eating, packing up their families. Others walked, filing past the train of nuns. They passed merchants selling every manner of goods along the road, and old bodies that had given out on the way to make a pilgrimage. Fathers trudged along with children who had lost mothers, and then there were children who had be deserted or lost the only parent they had , They became were orphans.

Sister Garnier insisted on taking them."After all we are supposed to be an orphanage" she said to the knights. She gave these two boys milk, and a rest in the wagon, then put them to walking with the others. A baby girl was the next orphan left by the side of the road. Sister Legasse took charge of her and fashioned a feeder out of a piece of Merena's sling, twisting the top and soaking in goats milk poured in one of the small wooden cups carved by Sister Authie.

The baby had lay in the hot July sun for a day as people

passed but was none the worse except for hunger and a sunburn.
Merena applied a cool potion to it as the wagon rolled, and the baby
slept on in Sister Legasse's arms. Merena was much better now with
fading bruises and soreness, but the mental images would never leave
her again.

This was the steeper, rougher terrain so McDowell took the
reins and tied his horse behind with the mule. Merena insisted Sister
Garnier take her place in the wagon for a rest, so she climbed on the
wagon seat with Mcdowell, and the boy from God's mountain.

"How far now?" she asked him as the wagon climbed upward
and the few still in the wagon held on looking at an impossible height
above them. They had been five days now. " We should be in
Andorra in a couple of days", he told her, "Sir Reginald tells me it is
at least another week, maybe two, but we are making good time even
with the children. In Andorra we will turn back northwest again and
go through many hills and valleys to get there. Of course, the Sisters
and you may find one of them to you liking and stop before then."

She shook her head," It seems to be everyone's wish to go on.
They seem to have respect for Sir Reginald's opinion that it would be
best for us. Of course they think you are wonderful too," she blushed
and looked out at the cliffs the wagon was bypassing. "How are you
feeling by now"?, he asked, "I noticed you are not wearing the
slings." She laughed, " It has been a rough ride but, yes, I am better.
The slings have better use now as diapers for the baby." He nodded,
smiling, "Yes, it seems we have an instant orphanage now. Is is good

in one way , as it helps all those who give a second look to ill- dressed nuns, like yourself."

"The nuns do take a vow of poverty, you know", she countered. She heard his stomach rumble as Sir Reginald rode by the wagon handing out the last of the cheese. The milk was saved for the children. "This is beautiful fertile country," she told him", the woods will have a wealth of offerings. If we can find game tonight I can make us a wonderful supper." "I will get the game," he grinned, "starvation does not suit me."

Sir Reginald rode up beside the driver. " Everyone is starting to lag behind. They are tired and have been going on little food." McDowell nodded. "We were just talking about a good supper, we all need it. Merena says she sees plenty in the area if we can get the game to add to it." She smiled at Sir Reginald, "I am sure tomorrow will be better with a night's rest and a good meal."

He took the lead again, scouting the less rocky path ,for the wagon, along the way He thought about the girl, what she had been through those many years, what she had done and was still doing. How she stood up to DeCaux and his henchmen, A marvel. Bravery was in her, as brave as any Temple knight. She is at her best when times are at their worst. If her people were all like that they deserved every chance to have the life they wanted. He would not be able to help the thousands that were in danger, but he would help these Sisters. He could see no difference between them and the many nuns he had escorted to Jerusalem, except that they were more grateful then the others who

took it for granted that they should be protected, fed, and
accommodated at every monastery and preceptory.' These women
make no complaint as they eat little and sleep on the ground each
night. In fact, they try to see to the comfort of we men and the
children, first. They surely deserve much better no matter what the
Church says'.

CHAPTER 27

1254, A.D. Somport Pass over the Pyrenees mountains

The border was near. A din of noise was heard as the crowd at
the border was gathering and those behind caught up. There were
soldiers guarding and questioning those who crossed into Andorra,
the only way into Catalonia. Some were turned back unless they paid
a bribe of some kind. Many were Jews who had been ejected from
France and hoped to find a home in Catalonia, or Spain. Some were
other undesirables, and the guards were also on the lookout for

criminals and Cathar's.

There were Templar's there too. Sir Reginald rode ahead to talk to them while the line of humanity was stopped. He would soon see if any messengers had gotten to the guards, calling for their arrest, for the actions in Carcasonne. He knew several of the Brothers there from the various Templar castles; Lleida and others in Spain ,all the way to Compostela in the South.

They each gave a sign of welcome. "Brother Montague", said one," I thought you went back to England a couple of years back, you have been missed." They shook hands. "I was called back to France with a hundred others to guard the inquisitors, especially one on his travels. You know the rebels are banding together and attacking in some villages. When they do they destroy all the written evidence against themselves".

The brother looked behind him, "The group I saw you with does not look like inquisitors. You must have gotten other orders." Sir Reginald nodded. " Yes , Brother McDowell and I did. A Group of nuns were sent from Toulouse to Spain to start an orphanage, many orphans left by the soldiers fighting, you know. They are bringing some along with them but I imagine they will need a large farm in Spain to feed the many they find in the villages. " The knight looked at the group of women. "Some are pretty old to be working nuns." Sir Reginald made a quick observation. " They are the teachers for the children.The Church insists upon it, you know, they work them half to death in the fields until they're of age. They give a small amount of schooling and a great amount of catechism in those years."

The Brother nodded. "I have seen it, I see they will have their own priest too, another old, devoted servant put out to pasture in the country?" Sir Reginald laughed, "This one still has many sermons left in him, believe me." The Templar knight said, " I do not like any of this, to tell you the truth, we are watching for Cathar's to take to Barcelona before they disappear in these mountains and valleys. It is an uglier business every year."

" I am well aware" said Sir Reginald. "It has escalated even more now, in England even worse for the Jews. I am to the point where I am not going to go to Jerusalem unless it is a direct order from the Preceptory Master, and not the Church." The other nodded. "I am in agreement, at least with the Masters we have an opinion and an option to say yea or nay."

He shook Sir Reginald's hand again. Bring your charges down this way and I will wave you through the guards line. "I am at the Templar castle in Lleida if you get a chance to come by." Sir Reginald waved as he went back to the wagon and told them to follow. He leaned over and spoke quietly to the driver and then told several of the women and children to get in the wagon. This was not a time for stragglers.

The trail took them through high hills and deep valleys, one as steep beautiful as another. A very few small villages on the way to Andorra, La Vella gave Merena ideas on what local fare was eaten there. They had to drive through the larger village, there were no other trails. Instead it was the wilds of mountain terrain with its forests, and valley lakes. They were one of many wagons and groups of people going through the village. They would not stop until they were away from it, so Merena asked Sir Reginald if he would buy two or three chickens in the market they passed. She also pointed out a few vegetables after she talked to a vendor at the village market .

Sir Reginald came back with a basket full. He sat it, and the tied chickens, in the wagon and they continued out of town. The excited children petted the chickens ,and looked hungrily at the food in the basket. They came to a large mountain lake that looked like glass reflecting each limb of a thousand trees. Not far off the trail was an open expanse of field hidden from view of the trail. "We will stop here for the night." Sir Reginald told them. McDowell reminded him the next day was Sunday. "It will be too dangerous to travel then", he added, "no one will be traveling that is not someone they are looking for."

"You are correct." said his Brother knight. "Then we shall rest tonight,and tomorrow. All need it badly anyway. Have we enough food?" he looked at Merena. " "Most definitely, Sir Reginald", she said , " Tonight we will have what they eat locally, a meal called 'Escudella', they told me about at the market. It is Chicken and these big tubers they had, and cabbage, leeks, and artichoke. I see some wild carrots we can pick too. We will have some left tomorrow, and I can find many other things to add to it."

" Look ye around at this fertile country. It is a market itself if you know where to look!" Her enthusiasm was catching. "I think

no king will eat better, then" chimed in McDowell, " and I am
starving. " She smiled in answer, but pointed to the open field. You
see those goats straying over there? I need a watchman. Soon it will
be time for the shepherd to gather that flock, and I need to borrow a
few cups of milk for the children and the baby."

McDowell looked at her in amazement.No wonder she had
survived on that mountain, this girl could, and would, do anything to
preserve lives.

A day, and two nights rest on full stomachs ,later they looked
refreshed and ready to tackle the world. They were back on the road
with only an occasional traveler passing them. The parade of pilgrims
had continued south from Andorra, while they were headed a safer
direction with little traffic to worry them.

It was still over sixty miles to Val D'Aran. A few more days
and they would be in their new home, a beautiful one according to the
brave Sir Reginald. Spirits were high in the group. they no longer had
to plod silently, maintaining their false identities. The older women
entertained the children with old stories and fairy tales. The younger
ones sang old folk songs as they walked.

Some sang hymns and beautiful chants unfamiliar to the
others. The two knights also sang a chant or two in perfect harmony.
It was a glorious sound in those male baritone and tenor voices
ringing down the mountainsides and echoing back. Merena thought
no angel choir could have given her chills the way those voices did
with the melodies. It made her think of the shepherds she had listened

to all those years on God's mountain.

"I did not know you knights sang so beautifully." She told Sir David. He blushed at his own enthusiasm to let go in this beautiful environment. "There are many ways to praise God," he told her, "In our castles, and preceptory's this is our way."

Father Simon climbed up beside them as the young boy got down and walked. "Truly beautiful!" he exclaimed, "The mountains here, the music, and this little congregation. No cathedral could praise Him any more. We may have left His mountain behind but we are surely in His house now. Look around you" he waved to all of them, " Have you ever seen anything as majestic?"

The remainder of that long day they walked and fell upon the subject of naming the baby girl that Sister Legasse held and cared for. Everyone had an idea and names flew around like the mountain doves. Finally McDowell hit on one they all,excitedly, agreed on. "You could call her Regina after Sir Reginald, who is taking her to a new life." There was hand clapping among the women. "Then Regina it is", said Sister Legasse as she burped the child. Sir Reginald just shrugged but several of the women noticed he puffed up in the saddle, and sat straighter. McDowell grinned, "Better than Davida".On the fifth day from the border they stood looking down into
the Val D'Aran, the valley of the valley. It was part Occitania and part

Catalonia and it was beautiful to behold. A narrow, but deep and long valley that ran for miles. They saw gentle green slopes that swept up into steep mountainsides. Slopes that could terrace for grapes or olives in hot seasons. The flat bottoms between the hills were field after field of tillable land that snow peak mountain tops looked down on.

There was silence as each one took in the sight;imaging a life there. Here and there they could see a dot of small settlement, and perhaps one, or more, villages. Many mountain lakes, streams, and one river were all evident, fed by the sparking water from the mountains. Here, would be no summer droughts as in much of Europe.

They were almost home. The younger of the group thought it would be a good place to live. Others, including Father Simon, had thoughts in another direction. He thought it would be a good place to die.

CHAPTER 28, 1254 A.D.

"How is your foot doing "? Merena asked Father Simon. I have hardly
had time to think of you." "I think I will do alright with just Sister
 Authie's walking stick.". he offered. They were mostly quiet as they
walked, and looked at the land that might be home. So much would
need to be done,
 Where even to start? Finally, Sister Garnier said to the ones walking
in front of her, " We have been so worried to get here we did not think
of what we would do when we did." Sir Reginald slowed his horse
down the steep trail and walked it beside her. "First, you must decide
on a place to settle as you look around. I recommend it be far enough
that you have no close people to you, but close enough to get
supplies."

     " We have two months to build a shelter big enough for all of

you, while others of you must plant Fall crops to feed you. Two

months before it gets cold, rainy, and snows. We must not forget that

any longer and nobody will come in or go out of this valley."

     It seemed impossible to think of doing all that in such a short

time, and yet here they were, and had to do it. "Sir McDowell and I

will not leave you until it is done," continued Montague. If the

weather holds we must leave in October, if not, we will be kept here

until Spring."

     Sister Garnier reached up and squeezed his free hand resting

on the front of the saddle. "You will have saved many lives over and

over by then. You surely are God's servant." He said nothing, but he

thought the Church would disagree, would actually condemn him for

what he was doing.

Why was it so necessary to kill? How did that figure in the grand
scheme? And the girl...she was something special, maybe not what
Brother McDowell had told him, but something special anyway. She
knew so much, she did so much. If she was male, she could have been
a great knight of the Temple, maybe more. Both of us will probably
be reprimanded by the Temple but I could not see this treatment as
right. They burned that poor gentle Sister Authie for nothing, and
were going to burn the girl, too. As far as I am concerned , both of us
did the right thing. I do not think the Church has the power to do
anything but excommunicate us. The Temple would not stand for it'.

There was everything to see as as they walked , cattle, sheep,
goats, and a few oxen on the mountainsides as far as you you see.
"Look at what they have to graze on", Merena told them, "Their milk
will be sweet indeed!" Here and there was a stone hut with a few
animals fenced in beside it. There was every kind of landscape, from
little patches of flat grassy field to small rolling hills to straight walls
of mountain reaching to the sky

In the distance were tiny villages of three and four huts or
houses a stones throw from each other. Not far was a large stone
church tower that broke up the wild, raw country with a sure sign of
civilization. Merena thought it was beautiful with its huge bell tower,
what she could see in the distance, but it was like the old Roman
churches she had see all her life, from the Roman church. Sir
Reginald saw the look on her face . "You must not worry", he said,

"There are all peoples here, from Jew to Catholic, to Cathar. In
Catalonia they have long been a refuge of all. This will be good for
the women and children. This entire area to the coast is the same so
you can get lost in miles of it and no one will bother you."

She gave him a grateful look. "I hope you are right. It is a
beautiful land." She picked up one of the boys and twirled around as
she walked. "Is not the air wonderful? It smells like fresh hay, like a
sweet barley cake, like molasses on flour cakes, what little I can
remember of it!" Her enthusiasm was catching for the exhausted
group.

They were near the bottom, now, and the children began to
run and jump. The young boys rolled in the thick, lush grass. Father
Simon clapped his hands as they did. It was good to see happiness, at
last, in the children's faces. They had not been children for a long
time, maybe never.

They stopped at a crystal clear pond, one of many, and drank
right from the pond, getting cups of water for those in the wagon. It
was time to stop, look around, and decide where to camp that night.
All was open land, where they were, with pines as far as they could
see up all side of the many mountains. The next thing Merena
noticed was that the hillsides were full of stones from huge boulders
to small rocks the size of ones hand. And she saw the huts hand-built
from stone , some with wooden roofs, so a shelter would be no
problem.

Wherever they chose they would have to have stones removed

from the land in order to grow anything. She reached down and dug a
handful of soil. It was good rich growing soil and there was an
abundance of sunshine and July heat

. It was wonderful to see how much water was scattered in
ponds and small lakes everywhere, especially since it was known to
be scarce in hot summers. Here, there would never be that problem.
She looked up to the tops of the mountains with their snow caps,
grateful to see they would never have to worry about thirst here

Sir Reginald rode to the edge of a hill rich with trees close to
the pond. He dismounted , telling them it would be a good place to
shelter for the night. It was time for everyone to rest, and those in the
wagon to stretch their legs. Sister Legasse spread an extra blanket on
the thick grass and laid baby Regina on it. Even the baby looked
around, her blue eyes large with wonder.

One of the small boys pointed upward to a rocky point on one
of the mountains. 'What is those birds?" , he ask excitedly.
"Ptarmigan's", said Sir David, "I never saw those before I came to
France." "They are good eating", offered Sister Garnier, "very much
like chicken. We shall not be hungry here." Sir David was enthused,
"Really? I shall make some kind of bow and arrows, I use to be pretty
good at shooting. We will have them tonight if I have to hunt all
afternoon!" "And I will cook them!" added the Sister, "right in the
fire on the biggest leaves that can be found, better than boiling, you
will see."

Everyone was feeling good,. The one girl and all three boys

were off running up the hillside to explore, some of the women were taking out the few cups and bowls. Merena and Sir David were off in the close woods looking for trees other than pines, although Merena stopped to inhale the fresh pine air. She noted the many groves of them for the pine needles she needed. Her eyes went to the ground cover and she mentally noted plants she knew and some she did not. It would take awhile to gather and try out the new ones. Some she would just have to grow from the seeds she brought, as well as some vegetables. Down by the water she would find roots to go with the Ptarmigan, and no problem finding greens, but what else?

Sir Reginald tied the two big horses and the mule on the other side of the pond to drink and graze. Then he walked over to the blanket with the baby and watched her cooing and playing. The women were all walking around, looking at the mountains or busy working. A few went to the thick woods to look for nuts and berries, or to relieve themselves.

Sir Reginald sat down and looked at the embedded rocks in the mountainside. First thing they would have to do is pick where they wanted to settle, this was just one area of the vast valley. There were many miles of it, maybe a hundred or more. Wherever it was must be with the same stony terrain, so a shelter must be started immediately. At least there were many hands to dig and carry the stones to build a shelter. The horses and mule could pull the heavier ones for the base of the building.

It would take a long time to build such a shelter that would hold them all.' He sighed at the thought of it.' The baby looked at him intently and smiled as she kicked and waved her hands in the air. 'This child, named for him, would be the nearest he would ever have for a family. He would not have children of his own so he could at least build it a warm, safe house to live in.'

It was a busy afternoon after they all had rested. Some of the women gathered firewood in the forest and the children carried it downing to the clearing they had chosen. Father Simon walked very well with his cane, looking for fish in the pond, seeing many large ones. Fresh fish would be on the menu many days, he was happy to see.

Sir David made a bow from a strong branch and whittled a few rough arrows from branches. He used a thong of leather that held his knife sheath for the bow string. By late afternoon he had two Ptarmigan and another kind of bird, and they were being prepared for an early dinner as they had not eaten that day. "We shall have to drink water", she told a few of them, "I think my days of stealing milk from stray animals are over."

Sir Reginald smiled at her, "You will be close enough to buy it now, and we will find it somewhere tomorrow. The baby can have broth tonight, can she not?" Sister Legasse was cleaning the baby as he spoke. "I can mash up some vegetable in the broth too," she added " she can eat it if it is very mushy.".

Dinner was Ptarmigan, baked roots from the ground, water plants, nuts and berries. No other people were around so the women removed their blanket veils and spread them on the lush grass in a circle around the fire pit they had made. Sir Reginald gave a light warning about the brown bears that roamed these wild mountains, and Merena made a mental note to find something that would ward them off, besides a good fire.

It was a hot summer night with mountain breezes in the high valley. All slept well from exhaustion except the small boys who watched for bears.

CHAPTER 29

Toulouse, France 1254 A.D., The Villa

Edward I of Britain and Wales, and Duke of Gascony, has married Eleanor of Castile and awarded her money and land. Innocent IV continues encouraging his minions to find lapsed Christians and outright heretics and burn them at the stake. The Waldensians are the latest victims of his declaration, though no one is safe as long as there is a witness to accuse them.

Innocent IV has declared sovereign dominion over the entire world due to the Donation of Constantine, mostly believed to be a forged document from the eighth century. These are dark days and the violence continues through all quarters.

Meantime, the Inquisitor Bernard DeCaux has returned from Italy. The report states he crossed the Pyrenees border following a message from Carcasonne about the trouble at the prison. A group of nuns and two Templar knights were seen crossing the border to Andorra, and then they disappeared. He told the knight he had talked to, at the border, that the Templar knights were to be recovered as part of a plot that killed prison guards, and allowed many prisoners to flee from jail. They would all be hunted down and be held accountable.

The Inquisitor then told ten of his men to hunt them down. The guard told him it would not do any good because he had no authority in Catalonia. 'We will see about that", he told the guard. "Meanwhile I will send these guards to the Templar castle in Lleida to watch for the knights. I will also go, immediately, to the Preceptory in Carcasonne. Of course, the Pope will do whatever I wish, so these knights will pay, and these prisoners will burn. That I guarantee."

It is most advantageous that one of our Spanish sentinels has duty at the border. He has been able to usher many undesirables across by saying nothing at all to aid in their capture from the French side. This kind of assistance the Order will overlook since it saves lives already doomed.

The Knights Temple in Catalonia is in a protected area, and so are non -Christians for the most part. The Templar's serve at administrative Lords rather than warriors. In fact they have so much property to buy , sell, and rent that little else takes their time. If there are military matters to govern they must have the King's men step in as the warrior knights are fighting elsewhere.

There are many non-Christians living quietly in Catalonia blended in with Christians and forming a friendly society. There are free Muslims, and also slave Muslims from the previous wars there. Jews who have escaped or been thrown out of France live there quietly. They play a respected and important role there and certainly are considered more as citizens than the Muslems. They all depend on each other in business and prosperity. with Muslems owning property as well as all other non-Christians.

The property belongs to the Temple, and has for decades. Their job is to acquire rents and properties, and payments for each. this constantly increases the holdings of the Temple. France is catching up in properties though they still have a way to go. There are many Templar castles in each country, perhaps as many as a thousand properties in whatever country they are in. These include castles, houses, businesses , vineyards and farms.

In addition to managing them someone has to do the work to keep them going, and those are serfs, slaves, or free Muslems, Christians, and non-Christians. The owners or renters must pay taxes yearly, plus award something of value. It is an interesting order, Christian , warrior, monk, businessman, and sympathizer of the downtrodden. They receive great benefits of food and lodging, prestige, but they also support the Temple personally. They give the Temple a piece of property, sometimes all their property. Once a year they give a donation, and they promise a horse plus their armor upon their death. With the many soldiers killed in war the gains of the Temple must be immense, including all the property they already own.

Many other associates of the Temple do the same thing, including women who pledge a horse and their best garment upon their deaths. Sometimes they do this , among, many others, in order to be buried from the temple ,and on it's grounds. I have said it before, and I say it now. I would be very concerned that the Church will cast its eye on all this wealth. Perhaps this is why my own Order remains silent and uses its own funding. It needs no political partners to achieve its goals.

CHAPTER 30

1254 A.D., Val D'Aran, Catalonia, Somewhere near Vilamos village

Two days later the Sisters and their protectors had walked down the valley to find a permanent place to settle. They found it about three miles out from the small village of Vilamos. It was near the river Garonne with its clean sparkling water and an abundance of fish, where low slopes would be good for a grape arbor, and olive trees in good seasons. There was an expanse of two or three meadows and fields to have a cow or two, and plant vegetables.

The heavy woods on three sides were thick with all manner of plants and trees, including beech, fir,oak,holly, water violet and many fruit trees like cherry were numerous. On the fourth side, the river below. It was a high valley where eagles, red deer, lizards, and other wild life shared the space with butterflies , and wildflowers of all colors.

They had passed through the few villages on the way with the residents staring to see such a sight of oddly dressed nuns escorted by

two warrior knights , and several children scampering along. Why,
there was even a priest, or at least a monk with them. Who were these
strangers that did not resemble any nuns they had seen? Were they
Catholic, or Cathar? Waldensian's or Walloons? Certainly not Jews in
those clothes.

Village women ran to their friend's homes. Men just stared or
looked down when they passed. Best not interfere where your nose
need not be. They did not nod back to the strangers but some of the
men had doffed their caps to the knights as they passed by. Merena
saw a small store and barn where some supplies might be gotten, but
it looked like they would have to go to the largest village. Vielha, for
anything else. But that time was still far away.

Now they had to build a shelter and plant some kind of crops.
Merena had very few seeds with her. just those she had saved from
last year, and that would not be enough for this brood that had gained
more people.

They rested that afternoon and discussed where they would
build, where they would farm and where a small vineyard could be..
The low hills were not as rocky on one hill behind them but many still
would have to be removed. The higher hills were loaded thick with
large rocks and dense woods. They would not build directly in front
of that mountain because of threat of wild animals. Merena was
anxious to explore and see what she could find in food or herbs. They
built a fire pit in the open area and a latrine just outside the camp.

The animals were taken to the next open area where,

someday, a barn might stand for a cow or sheep and a goat or two. During all this activity a man or two, and a woman or two walked by on a beaten path that would take them to Vilamos or one of the other settlements the way they had come this day. They glanced at all the nuns and the children and went on about their business.

Mcdowell got a rabbit and a squirrel. While the women prepared them for cooking he went with Merena to the deep woods in back. She would try the steep mountain woods some other day. There they found nuts, berries and plenty of edible greens and wild carrots. There were orange and lemon trees still with ripe fruit, and apple trees that would be heavy with apples in a couple of months. Other fruit trees were there but none she recognized. She dug out something that looked like it might be wild yams. She bit in to the fleshy root and decided It would be perfect for a stew, somewhere between a turnip and carrot in taste..

Back at camp she borrowed Sir David's knife to help the others cut the vegetables and get the stew started. As they did, a man and a woman walked by carrying a bag of grain and heading toward the little village, Vilamos. Merena want out to meet them. "We are about to sit for a meal if you would care to join us." she said smiling at them. "We gotta be getting back to feed the animals, but we thank you.," said the man hearing a different accent, "you have a mighty lot of people here to be inviting more to dinner, are you moving here or just passing through?" Meanwhile, the woman watched the four older children playing at the edge of the mountain.

"We hope to live here and begin a new orphanage in the valleys". said Merena," You see we have several children already. The woman smiled at the baby on the lap of one of the strange looking nuns but said not a word. Merena could understand almost all his words but the language and his accent were different. He seemed to understand her fine.

"The church in Vilamos is Sant Maria", he said carefully, "no one is sure which Maria that may be though, so everyone is welcome, even the friar I saw walking with a cane." "Thank you," she smiled, "though I only know of one saint named Mary, although I am sure we revere both, sir. We come from A little village in France , in the Languedoc, so you see this is a good place for us to have our orphanage, so many children whose fathers were killed, mothers too The children are lucky to be alive ."

" Yes, certainly I understand," he said with a broad smile." I am sure you will be welcome here.There may be other children here, or coming." he smiled. "This is my wife, Jolanda. We have two grown children back in Andorra." They waved to her, and left.

The knights were watching carefully as Merena returned to the gathered group. It was time to eat and Merena related her visit with the strangers. "They seemed quite nice.They are from Occitania, but they speak a different version of the langued 'oc.

"It's Catalan", said Sir Reginald, same language almost, but different dialect and with a Spanish accent. Should not be any trouble understanding each other." Sir. McDowell nodded to his brother knight. "As you told me, they should meet acceptant people here, even Christians."

" We are not that different", said Sister Garnier, "We just do not accept the Church's demands for oaths or priests, we do not hold with confessions to other humans.. These are not beliefs that should mean killing people. I think the common people know this. It is when the priests and inquisitors incite people to mob then they really have little choice. As I have seen , it would then cast suspicion on them not to participate. I do not think many people, if any, are strong enough to behave differently."

She took the baby from Sister Legasse so she could eat . She let the baby suck milk off the cloth they had used for her. Sir Reginald stopped at a farm on the way and bought cow's milk for the children, ignoring the faces of the farmer when the big knight asked for milk. "I have seen it, Sister Garnier", said Sir Reginald ," we just saw it with Sister Authie, no one there knew her. I saw women in the crowd with tears in their eyes. They saw she was out of her mind with terror. I never want to see that again."

McDowell felt he had to change the sad subject. He dug into his stew with one of the wooden pieces they had carved for use as a small shovel -like piece that could rake food to the mouth, and then they drank the broth. "First thing tomorrow we start moving rocks from the mountain and piling them in one area. That is what we have to work with to build this shelter.

We will have to get tools to build a roof, plenty of trees but it takes lots of work" .Sir Reginald thought of all the work ahead of them, and only the two men. The women could mix the clay and maybe even haul it, but none of them were strong enough to do much from the years of limited nourishment.. He secretly doubted they could get anything decent growing before winter

The baby was crying on her blanket and Sir Reginald went over to pick her up. Everyone stopped eating to look at the big knight walk out of camp jiggling the baby in his arms to quiet her. It had been a long time since they had even had interaction with a man around, much less seeing one with a babe not his own.

After they ate there was activity in the camp until bedtime. They cleared up the supper mess, swept the ground with their homemade broom. Sister Legasse washed the baby's spare diaper and few pieces of clothing. Sit David joined the other knight and Merena explored with two other women. The view from the high valley was breathtaking. They watched a herd of sheep being shepherded down the mountain pass to the river where they joined a few other cattle. Goats in threes and fours climbed higher and hung like pine needles to the edges of grassy cliffs.

Merena walked the wild fields that were the flattest and possibly. the most valuable in the area. It was plenty to have for their crops and extra to sell if they could. There were enough of them to pick all the fruit they could find to eat and also sell. So much was needed, a fire pit close to the shelter, a stone oven outside to bake bread, a decent private use for body duties off from the house , and

yet safe to use at night.   All the women had ideas and were eager to
make a home,at last. Their biggest fear was a bear.

Father Simon asked for his turn holding baby Regina when the
men came back into camp. One of the other women was busy cutting
and bending branches into an oval shape to weave a temporary bed
for the baby. Others were gathering tall reeds and grasses to weave
baskets and light weight containers. It was just the beginning of the
things they would need.

They worked by the light of the fire as darkness fell. Father
Simon entertained the children with bedtime stories while the others
listened to the noises of the summer night until they slept.

CHAPTER 31

1254 A.D. Val D'Aran, Catalonia

Sunrise sprang out of the mountain mist, and Sir
McDowell's moving around woke the others. There was no breakfast
except the nuts and berries left from the night before ; which were
mostly eaten by the children. They were rounded up by the knights,
who saw that they washed their faces down at the river. Then the
knights set set to removing rocks from the lowest incline of the
mountain that had the most limestone rocks jutting out of the earth.
Some would have to be loosened by a knife.

They had removed a few medium sized rocks when they

turned to see a large group of men and women coming down the path
from the area of Vilamos. They carried picks ,shovels, and other tools
The women carried all manner of food in wooden dishes and joined
the Sisters in the camp.

The man and wife Merena had met the day before came over
to her and said they had brought help. A group of men went to join
the two very surprised knights on the mountain and some went to the
next low hillside to dig out stone. They passed the stones down the
line from man to man. Soon the entire field was covered with
limestone rocks matched in flatness,and size from large to small, the
large for the bottom of the building.

When they had enough to start start building, each group took
a break and everybody ate. All the food sat on the ground on blankets
and each man ate from a bowl, washed it; handed it to the next man,
and went back to work. There were so many dishes to try that the
children ran from one to another with their bowls. All were fed ,with
plenty of food left, and they started back to work again.

The couple asked Merena to talk to the knights and decide
what size the building was to be. "It will be an orphanage and a
convent, " she told him. "We intend to build one large room with
many small ones for bedrooms for the women. The large room will
be for gathering. We hope for a second room or building for a
dormitory someday, and barn or stable for some stock. At least a cow
and a goat or two. I will see if the gentlemen are in agreement with
this." She thanked them for all the help and the food. It would never
be thanks

enough but all the women were so grateful and excited. They joined the lines carrying the smaller stones. All wanted to help.

Two men took charge ;called for the size stones they needed and walls started going up. They sent others to the river, and the mountain, to tote large amounts of clay. It was mixed thick with soil and brush to close up the cracks in the stones. Soon a doorway arch was seen. The sisters clapped their hands when they saw it was really happening. They had to chase the children out of the archway and let the men work..

The building began to take shape, a large rectangle with a doorway on each end and a large window area for each side. A second building was started beside it and a small stone building was started yet further behind. The men had to go higher on the mountainside to get more limestone rock. They rolled most of them down the mountain to retrieve as needed.

The four older children were sent to play in the first stone building to get them out of the way. Two men were building a large stone pit in the front of the two side by side buildings. It had a high back to control fire , a top and bottom ledge to hold pots.

There was little speaking during the morning and afternoon. The new neighbors pointed to what they needed, although 'Oc' was uttered many times. It was Occitan for 'yes', which everyone seemed to know.

Finally. the work stopped. Just as quickly as they had come the men picked up their hand tools and left without a word. The knights called to them; but they gave a wave and went on.

All the food had been left where it was and it was plenty for their dinner. The women looked around at what had happened in one day. Tall stone walls in the house ,and orphan dormitory, a nice size stone shed for storage or cattle, and a firepit for cooking and baking. It was more than they could have hoped for. They stood around the fire pit in a circle and offered thanks for this blessing.

The knights were exhausted but they all moved inside the first building to sleep under the stars. "Tomorrow we will start on the roof of this building" they heard McDowell say,". We will have to fell trees on the mountain and have the mule pull them down the side, but I have no idea how we will make timbers without any tools". Sir Reginald was asleep , snoring, his head on his saddle.

They were up at dawn drinking some kind of hot drink Merena had made with spices she found and added to the roots she had dug up. Everyone's muscles were sore so movement was slow. The strong, spicy drink seemed to help muscles in full complaint from the strain..

Then around the bend came the same large group of men carrying their tools! This time they had axes and two large home made saws that took two men to use , dragging the saw back and forth.. Women followed with more food. The sister's ran to them thanking them, and the knights stood to greet them shaking their heads and laughing. Now they would have to use the two horses as well as the mule to haul the logs .

It was not long until a load was next to the building being cut to size and fitted on the stone to central posts in the middle of the building. As the logs came the work went fast. A few men at a time stopped to eat then returned to work. By the end of the day all the buildings had roofs and partitions separating the main rooms from bedrooms. It had become a small farm in two days. Among many thank you's the men marched off ,again, to their own homes.

There were no floors but the women had gathered the sweet woodruff and rushes for the ground. Beds and tables could be made later. The buildings were strong and solid, would be cool in summer and warm in winter. For now they all had a new home thanks to wonderful new neighbors who thought they were a convent, complete with their own priest., or monk at least.

In the days that followed Sir McDowell decided to buy a cow and a goat for milk from one of the good neighbors who wished to sell. He also bought a bag of flour from the village so the women would not have to grind a huge amount of grain from whatever grains they could find. With the game he provided, including the traps Merena set, they would have meat, bread and butter plus what else could be found in the mountains. When he had built a pen, they could get a few chickens and raise more.

The younger women worked in the two large fields with Sir Reginald, removing scrub bushes , rocks, and weeds. Sir Mcdowell joined them to dig furrows in one field while the horses, mule, cow and goat grazed in the other field., cutting their work in half. The older women cooked, baked the bread, and watched the children, who were old enough to work but they gave out sooner. They helped to plant the seeds where Merena showed them . She tied a different colored snip of cloth in each area to identify where each type of food would grow. One day ,they would return a feast for to village who helped them.

The two knights and Father Simon had already had requests from men and women who helped them, to come and give advice, solve disputes,and keep watch for theft at the village market each week. This they did gladly, and with absolute refusal of payment offered. They were asked many times about the oddly dressed nuns but their answer was always the same, they were told the nuns were 'sisters of poverty', which they surely were. Finally, the closest thing to a mayer said to Father Simon, "Friend, we know you have been a priest,you wear the cross, but you cannot convince me these women are Catholic nuns. Do you not know there is a mix of people here? These villages have Jews, Waldensian's, Cathar's, and yes, Catholics. We live peacefully together , and some even go to Santa Maria church. The people who came to build your farm are,also, people like your 'sisters of poverty'.. The only wrong talk about them here is of the Mother Superior at the church. She comes once a week from Vielha with the priest, I do not even think the priest minds who his flock is. But she is complaining about these women dressing as nuns."

Father Simon nodded, "I can well imagine, however you might tell her that , in reality, they are Sisters in their denomination, and a more Godly group of nuns you will not find. To pass as nuns of poverty is how they survived sure death at the hands of an inquisitor. They saved my life on God's mountain, and I would give my life for them on this mountain."

The mayer slapped him on the back laughing heartily. "Oc! ",
he said in the Occitan language the Sisters knew so well," Yes! Well
said, my good Father. Well said! They are welcome here in hopes
they do not bring trouble upon our little village. I know of a few
orphans begging food in the mountains, I will get the word out as I
can. They must be exactly as you say to win such devotion of those
Templar knights. Everyone in the village is talking about them."

That night Father Simon related the conversation to Merena as
they sat on a rock watching the stars. They had not had time to talk
much the last few busy days. " You seem to be walking very well
now, just using that cane", she said to him. "Oh my, yes, it is hardly
tender at all, you did a good job with very little to work with. I would
put you against any Breton doctor, they only want to bleed the life out
of people." he laughed. "Well, Merena it seems the village is accepting
the women as part of the fold, now, except for a few naysayers."

"They do seem to be welcoming people, and how can we
ever repay them for building the orphanage?" she asked him. " It really
was remarkable for them to bring the foods, and the tools and work for
two days. The women seem to have found a peaceful home here, and
the orphanage just started by itself." Father Simon put his arm around
her shoulders, "Yes, but we must be careful of the Mother Superior,
the mayor gave ample warning about her. I have known a few others
like her through the years, she will not be as forgiving and acceptant
as the people in the village."

Merena nodded, "Perhaps I should visit her and tell her about the orphanage.She surely could not object to it". He shrugged, "Remember, she would teach quite a different religion to children." Merena objected, "I think the only religion the sisters would teach them is the Golden Rule. We think it is enough for anyone. It is the closest to pure gnostic thought from the first disciples that can be found."

He squeezed her shoulder, "I agree, but she would not. Just be careful." Merena suddenly had a chill. "Remember, Father, what you told me about the others? Jongleur and Emmalena? You talked about their dreams and visions?" He nodded, looking at her concerned face. "Well, I can't say I have had visions but I have dreamed about things that happen. I dreamed about this nun, I dreamed about Sir McDowell, I dreamed about this place too, and I dreamed about that inquisitor. I saw all their faces plain as day."

"Oh," he said, "I thought it would come, it seems you dream about what gives you the most emotion, that would make sense." "But it doesn't make sense to me , at all!" she persisted, "How would I see their exact faces before I met them?" " I do not know." said Simon, "any more than I know why the others did, but I know it is a gift, and I know they each used it for good, just as you will."

"But the knight? He is almost an enemy, I know he left everything to help me, but he is one of THEM. I could never trust him, I do not know why he has come this far." Father Simon smiled in the darkness. "Can you really not imagine why he is here? Why he risked his own life, his position and reputation? Not to mention his time, and now ,money."

She jumped up, "Is it not what some knights do? You surely cannot mean it was all because of me,can you?"

"Well well, yes, I guess I can. I have seen him and I have seen you with him. What is your thought? Why do you suppose you saw him in a dream?" She paced in front of him, "I just do not understand any of this, or what I am to do." He sighed," I can only remind you who you are, the Magdalen had visions ,we are told, how do we know she did not have dreams ,too, to help her along, and so it has been with your family. I might mention, too, that in Jongleur's story it was clear that Templar knights venerated Mary Magdalene as goddess. Sir David has not said any such thing, but I watch him look at you when you do not see it. Almost as if he is studying you. Just as it has the last few months, these things, perhaps, will come to you as you need it. Emmalena healed with her emotions, it looks like your actions will be used that way too. Look at what you have accomplished so far, you have saved my life, the lives of all the others, and now these children, and perhaps many more will be saved because of you. It all stair-stepped from you, don't you see? I'd say your gift is serving you well."

The next day was Saturday, usually a day when the Sisters spent quiet time doing quiet jobs. Some wove baskets and small dishes, some picked wild flowers and made bouquets. Others gathered herbs and flowers that Merena had taught them to find it each season. Some just used what time they had alone to reflect on their

lives and what they had lived so far. Many gave praise in their own
way, or devoted their time to thoughts of Sister Authie. Even giving
thanks to the two knights who had done so much was done often..

Merena wanted to be alone with her own thoughts. She
planted herbs from the bag she had brought with her. It was quiet ,and
the soil was fertile behind the stone barn the cattle used. This is where
she put her herb garden, the thyme, dillseed, rosemary, celery seed,
and so many others at one end, and the ones she used for medicines at
the other. She built a low rock wall around it to keep the animals out.

The knights were working in the field, gathering the wild
grasses for animal feed, needed to last through the winter ice storms.
Winter. Perhaps they would leave soon and go back to their lives, their
civilization. They would be missed by the women and children, not
only for all they did, but what they had become. Friend, protector,
provider, councilor, even disciplinarian for the children sometimes,
who listened to them more than they did the women.

'Would everyone really have a home here?' she wondered
'peace and happiness in this beautiful high valley so far from
everywhere . Is the orphanage even a good thing to do given that they
are hunted people? What would happen to the children if they were
found and arrested? They had gotten away, and now it looked as if
they had wonderful neighbors, except for the Mother Superior from
Vielha. Merena made a mental note to go see her on Sunday. Surely
friendship was the only way to insure there safety. Surely the nun

must have a good feeling about an orphanage.'

CHAPTER 32

12 54, A.D ,Vilamos, Val D'Aran

The two knights took the wagon to Mass on Sunday so Father
Simon would not have to walk. Merena went along to see if she might
have an audience with the Mother Superior. There was no activity
except at the beautiful church . She listened to the bells chime in the
tower as the people of the village went in. Some smiled at her and
some did not. The knights were greeting people at the door when the
Mother superior climbed the steps. She stared at Merena and cut her
cold with a scathing look. She gave a brief nod to the knights and
walked in like a queen, refusing the arms they extended to escort her.

The door closed and Merena sat in the wagon in silence. She
decided to look for herbs as she waited .and walked through the little
village to its outskirts. It was a beautiful place. She looked out over
the valley deep below her, and the snow topped mountains above her.
They were so close around her she felt like she could almost reach up
and touch the top of one. It was a high valley with a fast river below,
in constant motion over the rocks. There were high waterfalls she
hoped to see when there was ever time ,in days that were busy with
living. Soon it would be winter. She could imagine the giant icicles
that would grow ,from moving water, and the iciness here, Could they
ever be prepared enough for that time?

The bells were starting to chime again. She hurried back to the
wagon. The knights were talking to villagers after the service . She
knew they would be anxious to get back and do whatever it was they
wanted with the rest of their Sunday, so she told Sir David she would
walk back, she wanted to mention to the priest and nun about the

orphanage so they would pass the word. They drove off and she waited. Soon the Mother superior came out with the last few villagers. Merena waited until the conversation ended. "May I have a moment of your time?" she said to the Mother Superior. "I have no time for heathens." the nun said and began walking to the parsonage next door.

"Wait," Merena said abruptly, "please, I do not know what you mean. I only wish to tell you of our orphanage so that you may tell others, there must be a great need for children's homes as there is so much war in the many countries that are close to these mountains." The nun turned to her, "And you think I would send any child to you devil worshippers? Better that they should die from starvation than live with heretics. Even better that they should burn. The Bishop of Urgell is coming to this area next week, I intend to tell him about your group of women, falsely wearing clothing as if they are the holy habits of nuns, so I have been told! He will know what to do about you. I do not think we will have to suffer your existence very long in this, or any other,village."

Merena stood in her way. "I thought we might be friends and even work together for the children's sake. The villagers have been so kind to us, we are so grateful." The nun laughed rudely, "The villagers are sinners who come to church for penance, they've been told their penance will be great for helping the Devil's spawn."

"I feel sorry for you", Merena said quietly as the nun stomped off, but Merena's voice followed louder, " We, too, are Sisters of God.

We obey the Golden rule, but I see you do not. Perhaps we do pray to
a different God, because ours would surely be disappointed in your
words." The nun kept walking and called behind her, "Your kind is a
disease upon this land, get thee behind me Satan woman." When she
related the words to the knights they shook their heads, "She was not
very happy with us, either. I would not worry too much about that old
hen", Sir McDowell told her, "The Bishop may not like it, but his
power is somewhat limited here. He has power over his own diocese
but not out of it. The Church has just ruled that this year, as so many
Bishops were taking church and legal laws into their own hands. " Sir
Reginald expressed regret, "He still has a guard , much like the other
inquisitors in these times, though Aragon and Catalonia are pretty
much hands off, that is why the refugees come here. It is a good place
to get lost. Perhaps I should have taken you south where the Cathar
castles are. At least you would have had your own church to attend. I
am in great hopes the the people of Vilamos have accepted the ladies
and children. They did not have to build this farm but they did in spite
of the church many of them attend."   "I hope you are right," Merena
told them ,"but she was pretty firm on making trouble. You spoke of a
church for us, actually our church is where we are , wherever our
people are. In fact we will have a meeting tomorrow if you would care
to attend. None has been possible until now, I think you might find it
interesting."

Monday came, a hot August day that the mountain breeze shooed away. After the busy work was done and the day was ended with all fed , which included each ones work on the various chores of making furniture, planting seed, taking care of children and animals . It was time to start an evening fire in the new stone fire pit where bread would be baked for the next day. Sister Garnier called a meeting to order and all work was ceased, though the knights continued their own projects. One whittled a chair leg quietly, and the other polished his armor.

All sat in a circle but for the men. Sister Legasse rocked baby Regina while an opening prayer of thanks was given for the new buildings and the other good things that had come their way. Then began a round of each woman giving her individual thanks and praise, most of them including mention of the knights who had done so much. Finally Sister Garnier called for the memory keeper. Merena moved to the center where all could see and hear. She sat cross legged on her blanket , took a deep breath and closed her eyes to speak. Indeed, she might have been in a trance as her voice took on an otherworldly singsong tone. . Or maybe she was just concentrating intently to do her job. Her voice rang out across the valley and echoed back.

"To all worthy women in name who lived before, whose blood we share, who live in lore,

We honor and remember your works,your lives, as you helped God's word to survive

Across the waters to this fertile land, with sons and daughters
in your loving hands,

The Sarah's, Maria's, and Martha's we adore, the Tamar's, the
Miriam's ,so many more,

Namesakes, daughters who led us all ,from dusty Palestine to
verdant Gaul,

They held the truths we now pass on, that give us strength to
face each new dawn,

The troubles of Ruth, the strength of Tamar, and shining
Stella, our bright morning star,

The Naomi's that led with wisdom so true, our most revered
Magdalene, we honor you,

Joanna's devotion, in each saint we rally, to keep kith and kin
close to heart in this valley,

The Bethany's and Anna's who have gone before, the
Emmalena's have opened a door,

Wherever we flee, wherever is home, your sacrifices forever
be known,

We will persevere as we minister to all ,teaching, our healing,
whether we rise or fall,

We protect the bloodlines we each share, and the times of
adversity we all must bear,

Our harvest is mere survival, we sacrificed many, Magdalen
suffered more than any,

She is honored in each women since, her love greater than

anything to repent,

Our men who fought to keep us safe,are now in the beyond,
through Heaven's gate,

Those who strike us must call hate their own, for those burned
need no flesh and bone,

They suffered from the sword and lash, their spirits soar
through the fire and ash.

We remaining must pass the test others have done,then
eternal rest will come.

Each woman must be her own conscious guide,only she has
the inner know,

That will pass along our ancient pride, and help her generation
grow.

Matilda's, Hagar's, Melisande's too, each gives us grace to start
anew,

We heard of Juditha and how she could heal, the messenger
Jongleur we , now, know was real,

Good Simon's years have honored a deed, given us great
friend ship in our time of need.

 And Emmalena we now hold so dear ,taught us 'first daughters',
indeed, are still here,

The enemy surrounds us as in times of old, yet they cannot
erase the spirit we hold,

It resides not on Earth or in the grave but in each woman who
deserves our praise

Now our Templar knights have Heaven's reward, they chose
kindness, and not the sword

As we think upon each life in glory, remember we are
tomorrow's story,

Of all past women, in life, love and deed, they planted the
tree, we must sow new seed.

Now was total silence as the fire crackled. in the quiet. Both
knights had long since stopped their work to stare at Merena. There
was an electricity in the air that was so powerful the fire rose about
the high stone back of the pit, and had to be beaten back with dirt
thrown on by Sister Garnier..

Merena went off to be by herself as the group broke up and
quietly retired to their blankets. Sir Reginald asked to hold the baby
before she was put down. She smiled and cooed at him , patting his
weathered face with her tiny hands.

McDowell found Merena sitting on a large rock just outside
camp. "You should not be out by yourself, bears around you know".
She just smiled at him. "I know, but it is so hard to find any time
alone. " "Well come on back in the camp, I won't bother you.
Everyone's gone to bed anyway."

"Sit with me, if you like", she told him, "this is the time of
day I like, looking at the stars in this huge open place. It's like I am
the only person in this big wide world, and stars are putting on a show

just for me." He took off his sword and sat down. "We learn about the heavens, you know, the Templar's of the past were great mariners and navigators. Your name, Merena, it means 'of the sea' does it not? "

" Yes, so my Mother told me, she must have had the Magdalen in mind when she named me. It is said she was of the sea and came to our land. You know, she tried to tell me hidden things before she died but she was too weak, and I did not understand anyway. She must have known all along and that is why she taught me so much in the woods".

His body was very close to hers. She could feel his body heat and masculinity. "Did she teach you those memories?" he asked. "Yes, each memory keeper adds more in their life, I guess that is why it is so long, my Grandmother must have been a first daughter too."

"It was amazing to hear, I do not how you can remember it all. You realize it is very hard to understand what you are, no, who you are?" " I know exactly how strange it seems", she countered," since I only just learned from Father Simon a couple of months ago. But so much of it makes since now."

He leaned toward her, shoulder touching. "Yes, Simon said you were the descendant he had been looking for many few years. He said you had abilities that others do not have. May I know what they are?" He was too close. She stood up and struggled with her answer. "It is just healing knowledge, I think, but I guess, like Jongleur, I can see some things." "What things?" he asked. "I try not to see them so instead I dream them sometimes. I saw this place but I did not know where it was, I saw the Mother superior,   and I saw you before I met you." He crossed his muscular arms and leaned back on the rock. "It seems you saw things that would be important to you."

" Well, you and Sir Reginald have been very important, you saved our lives."

"Perhaps, but did you dream his face?", he offered, "No," she said honestly. "I dreamed of you too." he said, "Oh, it was after I met you, when you were my prisoner. That night, with my back toward you I dreamed I would set you free and take you home to Scotland with me. I dreamed I would keep you safe so you would never be afraid again."

"Is that why you got me out of prison?" she asked, glad he could not see her blushing. He leaned closer, "I was still fighting with myself about you. When I saw what they did to you and what they were going to do I knew I would never let that be. Then the rest just happened, you know, and here we are."

He stood up, beside her ,with his arm around her shoulders. "Look up there", he pointed, that low star, that is Mercury, it is usually a quickening of some action. . And that star is Venus, that's the sign of the goddess," he said, "Seems pretty fitting to me." He tilted her face up to him and kissed her gently. "I think you are a goddess," he murmured, "even if you are a heretic".

She broke away, "I think that kind of prejudice is how we got here," she spoke sharply and headed back to camp. "That is not what I meant", he followed her. "The goddess is sleepy", she told him, curtly, and went into the main building.

'Whew!' he thought as he went to his own night watch bedroll,
"that did not go well." He laid down not far from Sir Reginald,
"Scared her off, did you?" observed Sir Reginald ,as he turned over.
McDowell folded his hands behind his head and looked at the planet
Venus, "Guess so", he said. Sir Reginald yawned, "You know,
everything about this would complicate your life, but you would be a
very fortunate man to get her,Brother McDowell. Are you prepared to
stay here and fight to keep her alive?" The young knight thought a
minute and sighed, "I think I was prepared to even back on God's
mountain."

CHAPTER 33

1254 A.D. Close to Vilamos

Merena spent the rest of the week gathering all the roots and
herbs they would need for the winter as it came early in the
mountains. She found everything she would need but honey. But the
mountains were known for brown bears, where their were bears there
must be honey. It was time to follow the bees. Honey was not only
great for cooking and baking, it disguised the bitter taste of
medicines. There was no doubt that with these children, and any
more, they would need medicines for colds and other ailments.

She tried to mark the spots she found plants with a bit of
ribbon on tall sticks in the ground. When the snow came there would
be no way to find anything, especially the roots used for
cooking .Someone must dig a winter cellar by the stone oven to store
roots, nuts, greens, and other necessities for winter. They could also
save fresh meat that way for all winter. 'Winter....'

' Would the knights be leaving?' she wondered. She hated to

see them go for many reasons. Their protection, their hunting , a
hundred reasons. They were making some simple beds and chairs, Sir
David had promised to build them a large table with puncheon
benches. David, had done so much already, they both had.

But they had homes to go to and should not be kept away
much longer. ' Sir David,... what in the world to do about him?' She
was drawn to him like the bears were to the honey, but it was all
wrong. They were from different worlds. She could not leave the
women here all alone with children, and he should not give up his
world as a monk warrior to stay here. There was no denying she had
feelings for him, after all he saved her life. He had saved all of them.
'No, she must send him away if he would not leave when Sir
Montague did. He would make a good father, she noticed him playing
with the children.' I would like a child or two myself , someday,, a
'first daughter' perhaps?' She smiled to herself thinking of it. But all
that would have to wait. Perhaps she would find someone here,
someone like.. .well, like him..

He joined her up in the woods to help carry her load back
down to the farm. Yes, it could now be called a farm, convent,
orphanage, whatever they wanted. He had a load on the mule of oak
and hickory to split for furniture, and for winter burning in the stone
oven. The women were baking bread and sweet cakes every week.
Finally , everyone was getting plenty to eat, They had done without so
much it was good to see the bloom of health on everyone's face,
especially the

children

The baby was now eating solid food soaked in broth or tea ,and was gaining weight. Though everyone held and played with her ,Sister Legasse and Sir Reginald were her surrogate parents, picking her up anytime she cried. She was thriving.

The week had gone by so fast. Merena was wondering what they could use for more sleeping pallets, they had all brought theirs in one stack but the children had none, nor did the knights. Maybe they could acquire some bags of rags in the village to make quilted pallets .Several of them needed to go with her and gather bunches of the sweet woodruff and trillium to restuff all the pallets. They would also use the sweet smelling rushes for the floors until they had wood floors. Also , Quilted pallets would add warmth to their beds in the cold mountain breezes. At least each building had a sunken fireplace that could be used for warmth in the coldest days. No one had clothing tat was not on their backs.

Dawn the next morning found Father Simon and Sir Reginald building a fire to make tea by the time Sister Garnier and Merena got up, followed by some sleepy -eyed children. They were drinking the tea when Sir Reginald put his ear to the ground. 'Brother McDowell!" he yelled, "Horses coming! Many of them!" Sir David was at his side immediately with his sword strapped on and his dagger in his boot. He handed the older knight's sword to him as they came around the bend. Twenty men were in the group led by a uniformed superior.. The women were running in and out trying to get dressed and gather the children.

The captain held out a scroll when they stopped, and Sir Reginald, the closest to him, took it to read. The captain said loudly," These women and children are all arrested in the name of King Charles, and the Church."

"On what charge?", demanded Sir Reginald. "Heresy" said the captain. "We were sent by the Bishop of Lleida to make the arrest. The Bishop fell ill along the way, we had to leave him in Vilamos. We are to secure the area until he recovers to begin the interrogation. We know of you knights. We cannot arrest you ,so you are free to go. Everyone else is under arrest!"

Merena froze in her tracks, but McDowell immediately went to her side ; put his arm around her protectively. "We're not going anywhere, Captain," he said. "These are our friends. This is their priest, Father Simon, I think you have made a dreadful mistake. Haul your men out of here before I get mad at a bunch of mercenaries scaring women and children."

The captain shook his head, "It's not like that at all, these are direct orders from the bishop. Your friends are heretics, the bishop says, and that could implicate you if you do not cooperate and leave."

"We are staying right here", said Sir Reginald," until this matter is straightened out. Are you prepared to arrest half of the village of Vilamos, Captain? People of various religions have found a peaceful home here, if you arrest this group you must arrest them all."

"In good time, Sire, " As the paper states, these are the arrests for today. Stand back, I will post guards at each building here. "

Sir Reginald buckled on his sword ;looked at McDowell for agreement. "We cannot stop your squadron from holding these women and children, but we stay to see they are kept safe. In the meantime I demand you send a messenger back to Vilamos for the bishop to see me."

The Captain dismounted, "Yes, I will do that, I need to know how ill he is anyway. He is at the rectory. The Mother Superior is there caring for him. She came along with him to see the prisoners." "Aye, I'll bet she did", said McDowell, "she said she would sic the bishop on these sisters."

"Who are you?' asked the captain, noticing the accent. "Sir David McDowell ,from Scotland. And my Brother here is Sir Reginald Montague from England." The captain gave a light bow. "Gentlemen, you know we are just following orders. I do not like it any better than you. If anyone knows how the Church works it is your brethren." Reginald nodded in reply.

The men dismounted and two guards, each, stood at the front and back of each building as everyone but the two knights and Father Simon were ushered inside. Sir David walked Merena after the others. "I will be right here," he squeezed her hand. "Looks like this is finally it ", she said, "There's nothing we can do now". Some of the women were crying. Sister Garnier just looked angry.

" Finally, we found a place we could be safe and happy- and do God's work for these children, " she told the knight, "and they still want to kill us. Even the children will not be saved from it, God help them. "

Sir McDowell looked worried but he patted her shoulder in
answer. "Do you think we will let that happen?" he told her. "You
think Sir Reginald is going to let them kill baby Regina?" She was not
convinced. "You saw how they do, how are you going to fight off all
these men? You'll get killed yourself, and we will still burn at the
whim of that nun and the Bishop!"

"Rest easy, Sister, something will happen that will change
everything, I just know it. And we won't let you down." She took the
baby from Sister Legasse who was crying. "I know you will not leave
us", she said fondly, "you have done everything, more than anyone
could have -and we will never forget it. Neither will God, no matter
what happens."

McDowell turned and left ; went back out to Father Simon.
The rest of the captain's men had blocked the dirt road on each side of
the little farm. The only way out was straight up the mountainside , or
over to where it dropped off into the river, and valley, below. Sir
Reginald offered the captain a cup of the hot spiced tea, which he
took. "I sent a messenger ", he said "he will be back before noon I
imagine."

"What happened to the Bishop?" Father Simon asked him.
The captain blew on his hot tea, "All the way from Llieda, he was
coughing. He became even more ill and we had to tie him to his
saddle to get here. He did not wish to stop until he got to the rectory,
Mother Superior rode in a litter pretty far behind us. She's there now."

Father Simon looked stern, "These women are Sisters of God,

as much as any nuns, they saved my life and I will do whatever it takes to save theirs, mark my words." The captain crossed himself, in answer.

The messenger was back in less than an hour. " Mother Superior says the Bishop is dying!" He said breathlessly." " She says to bring the priest for last rites, that nothing can save him now !" Father Simon stood up, "She is wrong, Merena can save him".

The captain stared at him, "Are you crazy, Father? The nun ought to know, She runs a nursing convent in Vielha." Father Simon pointed to his foot. "I broke this on God's mountain, had cuts with infection set in. You see it is fine now. She did all this with plants from the woods. If I were you I'd try to save the Bishop. It would look pretty good to your superiors. I will pledge my life for her."

The captain hesitated, then said to one of his men." Take them in the wagon, and take two guards with you." Sir McDowell jumped up, "If she goes I go too, and Sister Garnier needs to help her, time will matter greatly." "Go get her," said the captain., "but no one else leaves."

Merena got her herb bag while the horses were hitched,and the wagon pulled out with the three passengers. McDowell had jumped on his own horse. He rode beside the wagon while the two guards followed. They were there within a half hour, the driver leading them in to the rectory. Mother Superior stood in their way. "What is that evil creature doing here? Get her away!" Father Simon tried to calm her. "She may be able to help the Bishop", he said, "I stand for her."

Her voice shrilled at him. "You have brought a witch into the rectory! I will not allow her to touch him!" Father Simon raised his voice back at her. "You are wasting precious time, Madame, get out of our way, and while you are waiting- I need the usual items for the last rites. Get them, but.. we , hopefully, will not need them! Now go!"

They went into the bedroom where the Bishop lay. "Oh, my God!" Merena exclaimed. "Help me! He's strangling!". She pushed him into a bent- over position, his face purple ,and his hands and feet twitching. "Hold his mouth open!" she yelled to the guard. She reached down inside his mouth and pulled out a thick wad of phlegm that had completely cut off his air; he made a horrible noise as his body reflexed and found an intake of breath.

"Get more pillows" , she told sister Garnier. "He should not be laying flat, he can't breathe as it is." The bishop was not conscious but after the body calmed she asked someone to find another sheet.

"Have the guards find the largest kettle they have here, boil water and bring it here beside the bed. Sister, you know the Chamomile, the liquorice root, the Calendula, and the Camphor leaves. While you find them I am mixing the fenugreek, white willow, and yarrow. He is burning up. No, that's foxglove, he is too weak for that" . McDowell stood by nervously, watching these procedures.. "Here", she told him, " Mash these elderberries up in a cup, one over there on the table. Sister, help me hold him so I can pour this in him, I want to see if he chokes on it. I must get his fever down."

The two guards were back with a sheet and a blanket, and the boiling water. "Put it on the other side of the bed, right by his head." Then she took the sheet and threw it over the pillows he was propped against to form a tent over his head. The steam rose up and puffed out the sheet, which she tucked under him. "He is starting to breathe better already", she told Sister Garnier, "I want to let him rest in that steam while I try to get his fever to come down." Mix up those brittle Camphor leaves with the liquorice root. What can we use? We do not have any honey." "I'll go look for some in this kitchen" said McDowell. He came back with some in a bowl. "Is this alright?". "It is just what we need", she said, She made a thick paste with the mashed leaves and roots. "Can you remove his robe to his waist and smear this all on his chest, his throat and neck. I even want some on his back, if you can. Pull the shirt back up to hold it all in."

She checked under the tent and saw that his breathing was more even ; color had come back into his face. She tucked the sheet back under him. " I want to give him more of the white willow, and elderberry root, Sister, let's add yarrow to it too. Is there any garlic in there? Good. We'll give him this as it is, but I want to grind up more and add it to honey. It has to be thinner now. If he comes to, it will be easier for him to swallow in honey. Sir David, will you be in charge of greasing his chest and neck the next time? Right now there is nothing more we can do until we see if the fever comes down. I'm giving him another dose of it. I do not think one is enough at this point." "Why is he unconscious?" asked the knight. "His fever is too high, it is affecting his brain and shutting his body down" she said," I just hope I have caught it in time...the next hour will tell. He has a very bad infection. Oh, the water is cooling off now. We need another pot if you can tell the men to put it back on the fire, David. The Bishop needs to get some of the fluid out again, that is what strangled him. He has to be watched so it does not happen again. Right now he is resting easier than before, that is a very good sign, is it not Sister Garnier? But if the fever does not continue to ease up he is sunk and so are we." Sister Garnier held his mouth open while Merena got the medicine thinned with honey and water, in him. She massaged his throat which helped him swallow even though he was not conscious. Then they watched to make sure he did not choke on it.

Merena uncovered the sheet for fresh air until they came back with the water. She sat down on the floor beside the bed and waited. McDowell got them some weak ale from the kitchen, and drank a cup himself. Father Simon stood at the end of the bed making the sign of the cross , his lips moving with a prayer. Merena smiled at him when he was done. "More good medicine?" she asked. " I hope it is, it is a habit as strong as breathing itself", he told her. "You remind me so much of Jongleur, all those years he had his own way of doing things, his own connection to God." She smiled, "I hope my connection is as strong as yours".

The two guards were back with the water and sat it the same place at the head of the bed.. "Sir David, will you go ahead and grease him again before I put the sheet back on ?" While he did this Merena felt the Bishop's head and arms., then she covered him with another blanket, up to his chin. "Sister, can you hand me that quilt over the chair? " She wrapped his body tightly with it, keeping it off the sheet tent she had made. " Now he must sweat, and he must cough. If not, he will not last long." She sealed up the sheet and sat down again, grinding more elderberry root and fenugreek.

Suddenly Merena got up and paced back and forth at the bottom of the bed. She looked at the man under the sheet again, lying so still, and then she grabbed her herb bag. She talked to herself as she dug through the bag. "I know I have trillium root, and fennel seeds, do I have any milkweed? Yes there's some. Here's the thyme, I can use some of the Sweet William and garlic. We'll mix all that with more Camphor, some eucalyptus, that's all good. If I give him enough he should start coughing, everything together will help, maybe add more elderberry root. It needs to be powdered more. But how to get it in him? The honey will do, spoon it in little by little but do not let him choke on it. It's too thick that way, water it down, yes, if that will not do it , nothing will" . " Can someone get me a clean rag? His mouth will have to be cleaned out if he coughs, that stuff will be way too thick." She was mixing it all in the same cup with honey and diluted it just enough to go down like melted butter.

The guard at the door said, "The Mother Superior is at the door, she wants to come in." They heard her talking through the door to the other guard. "Is the Bishop dead? Has the witch killed him yet?"

McDowell went to the door." Mother , she is trying to help him. It's the most important time,you may not come in unless you remain totally silent."

They heard her move away talking to herself about'" how uppity the Templar knights had become, no respect for the clergy...".

Merena carefully spooned the liquid into the throat of the Bishop. After three spoonfuls his body reflexed into a gagging cough, and phlegem came out of his mouth as he was in the sitting position. They now had him propped on the bed pillows ...his body laid over them. She caught what came up with the rag so it did not choke him. Sister Garnier held his head.. "There's much more bound to come up , help me hold his head while I get it out. The noise he made in coughing told them all how much fluid he had in his lungs."That's a dead man's cough," observed Sir David, nervously. Father Simon shook his head, "No, we must have faith in Merena, and God".

Sister Garnier got on the other side while Merena reached in his mouth to scoop out more phlegm. That caused the Bishop to choke and cough even more, bringing more up. Finally, he calmed and she made sure there was not any obstruction. Sister Garnier felt his head and shoulders. " The fever's down!, she exclaimed. "It's down quite a bit!".

Merena felt his head too, then nodded. McDowell watched in amazement when she leaned him forward and began pummeling his back with her fists. The Bishop began to cough again, over and over. His mouth was slack and the foul colored phlegm came out on

the rag Sister Garnier held there. Merena check the color of it. They
leaned him back a little, then. "We will have to do that again, but let's
let him rest now."

They leaned him back over in the sitting position again so that
he was slumped over the pillows . McDowell saw the man's eyes
flicker when they did. "Is he awake?" he asked them. " Merena shook
her head, "I think it is just his body reacting to all the things I've been
doing".

"No..." the small weak voice said, he turned his head toward
her, his eyes barely open, but he saw her, "Magdalene? You are here?
You've come to get me? Oh, let me touch your sweet face."

His hand came up and fell back down, but he stared at the
face. "Beautiful angel... you have come", he said to the young face he
saw leaning over him. and then he began coughing on his own. They
wiped his mouth and when he stopped coughing they heard him say,
"God is so good", and went back to sleep.

"You did it!" ,said McDowell, his voice low, "He is going to
live, after all! " Merena sat down and drank her weak ale, "He is not
quite out of the woods yet, his fever may go back up very high, and he
is rather old to fight it, but he did come to. I am going to leave him
alone for awhile and let his poor body rest. Then we will go through
everything I gave him once again. Maybe you can pound his back for
me, and grease his chest . It's that fever and choking I worry about."

Sir David gave his chair to Sister Garnier. "I never saw
anything like that in my life", he told them. Sister Garnier smiled at
him, "In eight years many of our group has had the same illness,

haven't we Merena? But I think the Bishop's was worse. None of us strangled like that, Merena just got to him in time or he would be dead right now."

Sir David said, "I have seen many men die, but not strangling with their eyes popping out of there head like that, trying to get a breath that wasn't there." Merena covered the Bishop again, in the tent, leaving one small opening to watch him. "He has been through a bad time", she said quietly. McDowell looked at her, "He thought you were Mary Magdalene come to take him to heaven. A family resemblance?" She shrugged. "According to Father Simon it is. I am not so convinced."

Father Simon put his hands on her shoulders and shook them affectionately, " Girl, I saw, and knew, three of your relatives many years ago. You could be a twin to the beautiful Emmalena, and Jongleur, in looks,..and deeds."

CHAPTER 33
1244 A.D. Vilamos rectory, St. Mary's Church

In a few hours the Bishop awoke again. Merena had given him another dose of medicine for his fever ,and for the coughing. It was

the violent coughing that wakened him. Merena had gone to the little
kitchen to see if they had anything to make broth . Father Simon was
sitting by the Bishop when his eyes opened. "You are a priest?", he
said weakly. "Only a simple monk now," said Simon, I once was a
priest but I have been on a pilgrimage . You must rest and not talk
much, Your Eminence".

"Am I dying?" ask the Bishop. Simon patted his back, still
leaned over on pillows , his head turned toward the monk. "I do not
think you will now, you have been very ill, very close to death, but my
friend has saved you twice, now." "I thought I was dying", said the
Bishop," I saw the Magdalene, I thought she had come for me.."

Just then Merena walked into the room and his head twisted
up to see her. "There !" he said, he reached his hand for her and she
sat down with him. "Rest now', she said "I am Merena."

Simon said, " This is the young woman who saved your life
twice. When we got here your were choking to death. You would not
have lived through this illness without her medicines."

"You still need medicine and care, and you need much more
rest." she told him." He shook his head, not understanding it all. How
is it you happen to be here?. the Bishop asked. Simon , once again,
took the conversation. "This is the girl Mother Superior brought you
here to interrogate and arrest, Merena and her other friends. They all
were arrested by your men this morning. You see, Eminence, I knew
she was a healer, and then your captain let me bring her here to help
you. Mother Superior called her a witch but I assure you the
knowledge

she has in healing has nothing to do with witchcraft. She and her sisterwomen are as Godly as any nuns of a convent, and yet they are the ones you want to kill."

The Bishop looked at her and at Sister Garnier, who was wiping his forehead again.. His voice was very weak, ""Thank you, both, for all you have done. I could hear you talking to each other in my sleep. No one is going to harm you. I would like to sleep now, but when I waken we will talk more. I want to hear all about your group and what you are doing. I owe my life to you, young lady, and I would like to make a difference in yours."

She nodded to him, and his eyes closed. ' He almost wished that it had been the Magdalene coming for him, but there was much still to do. It was not yet his time, and this girl who looked like Mary Magdalene had been sent by God, to save him. Now he would save her.' He drifted off.

"I want to see the Bishop", snapped the Mother Superior, who had pushed the guard out of the way. "You may see him later, but he is asleep and resting now", said Merena. "It was lucky you decided to call Father Simon to you or the Bishop would not be alive. Because you did, I was able to help him."

"Hrumph!", she said as she skirted past them and looked at the Bishop. "Your Eminence", she called,"how are you?". He briefly opened his tired , sick eyes and said to her, "I will be fine, listen to me, I want you to leave them alone."

CHAPTER 34

Toulouse, France, 1254.A.D. The Villa

    `   It seems our sentinel in the Corbieres mountain area got a slight reprimand for the assistance he gave a group of heretics, and two knights who caused a big problem in Le Mur, the Carcasonne prison. Not only did the rebels in the jail escape but many others were freed and went underground ,however they could. I say slight reprimand because it saved the life of the one we watch. We continue to watch any member of that family. I hear DeCaux is mad as a hornet and vows to get his revenge. At least two of his henchmen were killed in the escape. He has doubled his guards at the prison, and his own guard.

        Speaking of DeCaux, -the master file keeper, the inquisition has been making bold steps forward. although there have been a few peaceful years it has never ended. It just became more organized these last years. In the beginning there was no single Inquisition. Instead, there were the individual tribunals of Dominicans, Franciscans, and local Bishops.

        Each tribunal had extraordinary jurisdiction and power. They were exempt from local law, and from episcopal control, subject only to the Pope. These tribunals waited for no formal accusations. Proceedings against heretic suspects were were held in secret. The suspects were denied an attorney or a notary such as myself. They were given no information about their accusers or the testimony given against them, whether their children, criminals, accomplices, or other heretics. There was no right of appeal at any sentence or decision. We have one tribunal here in Toulouse ,and one in Carcassonne.

Massive manhunts have been employed and ecclesiastical judges have claimed the right to proceed ex-officio against suspects now, with no accuser, requiring the suspects to purge themselves by oath or ordeal. This has been adapted to initiate action when there is even a rumor of any persons devotion to the Church.

There is a variety of tactics used to punish rebels prior to burning at the stake, thought I am sure that takes precedence in many areas. Shedding the blood is frowned upon by Canon law so other ways are utilized to gain confessions, find other heretics, or temporarily rehabilitate suspects for later inquisition. Sometimes prison is the starting point, many time five years or longer in chains, dark cells , and bread and water enough to keep them alive. These punishments allow the heretic time to think it over, to break them down, manipulate by torture, threat, or send their family begging for their confession and conversion.

The record keeping developed by those, such as DeCaux's, enables them to go back and arrest or investigate relatives burned, or in prison, sometimes generations later, grandchildren of former heretics are frequently arrested and punished for the 'crimes' of their ancestors, even if they are converts themselves. Those who do convert are always suspects.

The records kept are extensive about every person. In Carcasonne alone their are nineteen registers of names, fifty-six

books of investigation, three cahiers, nine rolls,plus many documents.
As I mentioned in an earlier report these records are kept under lock
and key so they cannot be stolen and destroyed.

Those who do not convert receive penalties that range from
whipping, mutilation, to execution. Those who confess receive
penalties of monetary fines, public infamy and shame, pilgrimages
lasting years, confiscation of property, or imprisonment. Should they
recant their confession they are burned,

A penitent heretic is set apart from everyone else in the
village, forced to wear yellow crosses sewn on front and back of their
clothing. The crosses must be two and a half fingers in breadth, two
and a half palms in height, and two palms in width. False witnesses
are forced to wear a red tongue.

When convicted the heretic's penance is never completed.
New penances can be imposed,or the old penances reinstated at any
time. Perhaps worst of all some heretic's work within the Inquisition to
find and identify other heretics, in order to reduce their own penance
or punishments. Even now, in Toulouse, many relapsed heretics have
been dragged from their prison cells and burned. It is a daily event.
One can imagine the stench that permeates the air. I do not go out, but
it clings to the clothing of those who use my services.

Given the above report is it any wonder there is an
underground exodus over the Pyrenees to leave with nothing but the
yellow crosses on their backs. Those who make it, that is.   This is a
human condition I am forced to watch, and share with a future time. I

can only pray that history does not repeat itself, that people do not kill their friends, neighbors, and citizens. It is up to future. Surely if how we have failed is known it will never occur again.

CHAPTER 35

Vilamos, Valley of the valley's, Catalonia 1254 A.D.

Merena stayed with the Bishop for the better part of a week.
At his order the guards took Mother Superior back to Vielha, and the
other guard took Sister Garnier back to the farm, where the women
and children were released and the soldiers returned to the village.
They would wait there to escort the Bishop back to Lleida. Between
Father Simon, McDowell and Merena they managed to entertain and
care for the Bishop.

When he felt well enough they tied his horse to the back of the
wagon and drove back to the farm as the Bishop insisted on meeting
the women after hearing of them, and their years on God's mountain.
He had a small escort follow them to take him back to Vilamos.

The Bishop was welcomed after they had heard all about him
from Sister Garnier. He had Merena's spicy sassefras tea after a lunch
of rabbit stew,.then he went into the two long stone buildings built by
the villagers, with the children pulling on his robes.

"You have no floors, and winter is coming!" he exclaimed.
the woman nodded, not saying they had lived without more than floors
the last eight years. He saw the mean bent wood chairs, the thin
sleeping pallets, and the lack of most necessities but said
nothing. They showed him the wild field they were planting with what

little they had, and the cow and goat Sir McDowell had bought them. He shook hands with the elegant Sir Montague who had given them so much, and told him he was God's servant.

As they sat in front of the stone oven drinking their tea he asked them all to gather around before he left. "Sisters", he told them, "I have heard all about you as I recovered from my illness. I have seen your strength , all of you to survive the times, and your spirit to gather these children. I wish to be allowed to assist you , though no more than these noble knights have committed to doing, these last months."

" I am going to award you twenty acres for your farm and orphanage, more later when you need it. You will have the paper deeded to the orphanage forever and may use it as you see fit, without fear of infringement or arrest. You no long will need to wear the faded apparel and pass as false nuns, for I will send many bolts of cloth for clothing for you, and all the children. There are many other things you need and I will send as many as I can the next few weeks. In the time I have talked to Merena I have learned many things. I have seen the value of the herbs and plants she used to save my life, and along with other crops it would be wonderful if they were grown on part of your land."

" You can also sell them at any market you wish ,to earn money for yourselves and the orphanage. I am sure more children will be sent to you so there will also be supplies for the children to have schooling, clothing, and food. I understand there are three teachers among you.   What do you say to this?"

There was din of excitement as the women thanked and
talked excitedly to each other. "I want to do this," he said, I am happy
to know that all of you will live peacefully, making homes for
children. There is just one thing I ask...if the children want to attend
St. Mary's of Vilamos, will you let them?"   They all instantly, agreed
to this.

As he mounted his horse the Bishop smiled at the happy faces
that had looked at him so fearfully when he came. "May I be welcome
at some future visit to share a meal and that lovely sassefras tea?"
They all voiced agreement and came to see him off. He patted
Merena's face, " I Thank God for sending you to me, to teach me, be
happy my child". As he rode off the three boys ran after him until all
the soldier's horses disappeared.

It was a happy time the next few weeks. The Bishop was as
good as his word. Every few days a wagon load came to the farm.
One of the first held wood planks for the floors and rugs to put on top.
The two men bringing the wagons were instructed to install the floors
and leave their tools behind for the sisters.

A wagon full of bolts of colored cloth, and threads, came,
something the women had not seen in years ,as they never had but
what they wove by hand. They could not keep their hands from petting
the beautiful colors. A wagon came with shoes, and beds, and
blankets, and toys for the children. One came filled with sacks of
grain and flour, kettles and bowls and cups. One with simple farm
implements and vegetable seeds. The last one came with basic chairs
for both

buildings, and wood to make other furniture. It took days to start using , or storing it all.

The two knights and Merena walked the land up hills and fields to determine the land they were given on the deed that came with one of the wagons. They posted sticks at each corner with colored cloth on them to mark their property.

Sir Reginald was busy building a tall chair for baby Regina when visitors from the village dropped in to see what all the wagons were bringing; what was going on. They were welcomed, women admired the cloth and the other items. They could not believe the Bishop had done it all, nor could the parish priest on his return. He had heard the whole story from the Mother Superior, but he did not come to the farm.

The Bishop had heard right about the teachers .. There were three former teachers in the group of women. There was also a weaver, a baker,, a midwife, a seamstress, several farmer's widows, a vineyard owner, gardener, and a deacon. of the Cathar faith.

There was a happy flurry of activity the next few weeks. The women were busy, sewing, storing, baking, planting, teaching, using the tools left, gathering more herbs to sort , making friends with villagers. They were busy living for the first time in many years. The children were busy playing, learning, doing chores. They were busy being children.

One night Merena went to sit on her great rock looking down to the river and up to the stars. She was wearing a new Robin's egg

blue gown the seamstress has made her. It brought out the sun
bleached reddish auburn of her hair and her blue eyes sparkled. Sir
David joined her after taking a shower in the outside shower he rigged
behind the animal confine. It was a large pot of water attached to a
rope he pulled to dump it. After that it was very popular with
everyone.

As they talked Sir Reginald came and sat with them. They,
each in turn, looked from the foamy rushing waters of the Garonne
river, rushing far below them to the snow capped peaks all around
them, set in a clear sky of stars so close it seemed they could reach out
and grab one.

Merena began a whistle of that chant of the shepherds she had
listened to so many years, and then she began singing the words in
her high, clear voice. Almost immediately she heard voices coming
from all over the Valley of the valleys return the beautiful song back
to her. It seemed there were many of them, all echoing through the
mountains.

When the last echo stopped Sir Reginald told them,
"Everything has been moving so fast I haven't had half a chance to
talk to either of you. The ladies seem very happy, do they not? Happy
and busy, with so much to look forward to" . "Yes, it seems like a
miracle after the past years, like waking from a bad dream. I still
cannot believe all the Bishop has done for us." she told him. Sir
Reginald became very quiet, but they knew his ways now by now.

Finally he looked at McDowell, "We need to be thinking of

leaving soon, Brother. I can check in at Lleida, at the Templar castle, see what they have to say about what we've done, then I need to get back to my estate in Somerset. I've been gone a long time." They both stared at him. Merena was the first to respond. "So soon? I had hoped you both would stay this first winter."

"I would like to, but I think everyone will be fine now, and the villagers are becoming more friendly every day ,if they are needed. The planting is coming along and the boys will be old enough next year to work in the fields." Reginald paused again. "There are some things I have not spoken of until now. Back in England I am not Sir Montague, I am Lord Montague, I have a Barony there. The reason I tell you now is because I have made a decision. I would like to take Regina back with me, and adopt her. I have no heir and would like to give her my name, and my estate when I die. She would be Lady Montague now, and Baroness Montague later. She will never want for income, and will have a fine dowry. Of course that means she will marry a nobleman, possibly even a Prince or King."

Merena's mouth had fallen open,"That's incredible!" she exclaimed, "What a lucky little girl she will be! Of course you may have a time getting her away from Sister Legasse." "I have thought of that", he said. "she is along in years. I might ask her to come along as nanny first, and then teacher." McDowell grinned from ear to ear, "Sounds wonderful! Good things just keep happening!" Sir Reginald stood, "Well, just wanted to let you both know,
I would not say anything to the others, just yet." He walked off, and

Sir David looked at Merena, "I should go with him, especially if there
is any trouble for what we did in Carcasonne. We do not have long to
decide when we go, either .It's already September."

She was very quiet . " I do not want to go", he said," I don't
want to leave you, Merena, I think you know how I feel." He turned
her face to him. "I have been waiting for some sign you feel the same
way. I want you to come with me to Scotland, be my wife. The
women and the orphanage will be fine here, but you never will be
safe here now that it is known what you can do. DeCaux will never
forget you and will hunt you down, no matter what. That nun will
never forget the slight from the bishop, she will take any opportunity,
and I know you can see it already. I want to marry you, and I want to
protect you. I can do both in Scotland."

She got up. "We will talk about this in the morning" she said
softly, " I am very tired, and that is not a time to talk about such
things." He nodded as she walked off. "In the morning ,then," he said
firmly.

But the next morning, just after dawn some of the women
were starting a fire in the stone pit to cook the children's breakfast.
The thunder of horses hooves could be heard from a long way off.
Before the sky had anything but pink and orange hues stretching over
the valley within a valley, a parade of a hundred horses , and men in
full livery were upon the farm entrance, led by four men across and
one woman wearing the black and white habit of a nun. It was the
Mother Superior riding side -saddle next to a familiar red velvet cape.

The leader was of Bernard DeCaux. He was red faced and already giving orders while some of the farm women shrieked for help. The two buildings were emptying of frightened women and children. The two knights came out of the main building where they had been stacking wood by the fireplaces ,to build up the fires for the chilly days ahead. DeCaux immediately climbed off his horse and began talking as he looked around.

"You are all arrested in the name of Pope Alexander, and charged with heresy. That includes the two of you too he spat at the knights. "Round up those women" he yelled at the first row of horsemen. "You there," he said to the next row. "Go find all of the children, help The Mother Superior gather them up until we see which of them are heretics. They all drew their swords, battle seasoned men who meant business with the orders they were given. Many of the women were just dressing . They were being pushed into a circle and told to sit down on the still frosty grass. The knights were looking around the confusion before their swords were taken away. A fighting stance would have been senseless against so many. They scowled at the men who had been comrades and brothers just a few months ago. "By whose orders do you dare to arrest us!" demanded Sir Reginald.

Decaux pulled a scroll from his cape. " "I need no orders to make this arrest. you should know that. I have chased you all long enough, and thanks to Mother Superior here, I have you now" .

McDowell, looked at the nun just as Merena was being dragged out of the second building. "You just could not wait to cause us all trouble, could you? You were bent on revenge because the Bishop lived, and he silenced you. You were angry, and this is the way you get even...!"he yelled at her.

"It was my duty," she countered back. "The children do not belong with that witch, with any of them. " Just then she went over and took the crying baby from a visibly shaken Sister Legasse. She went back to her horse and stood with the baby, Regina . The baby held her arms out for Reginald, screaming as loud as she could. He walked over to her forcibly took the child out of her arms.

"Get your hands off my child ", he said. "I am Baron Montague of England, and this is the child I am adopting. " The baby quieted down since he held her. DeCaux looked surprised. "I didn't know, he said gruffly. "but that does not make you innocent. These women are going to the stake, here and now, I have no choice but to remand you for a trial since you are a noble."

Reginald pointed at him with his free hand, "They all better get a trial,a fair one, or you'll have the British at war with you, the Pope, and your country.!"

DeCaux waved to two guards to chain him up. "Give the baby back back to its nurse for now", he ordered and Reginald let them give Regina back to Sister Legasse, who was sitting in a circle with the other women.

McDowell had gone to Merena's side and was staying with her. DeCaux motioned to about twenty knights." Count these

heretics, all the women, that one too", he motioned to Merena.
"When you get a number ,I want that many stakes in that field over
there.." Some of the women began quietly crying. Both McDowell
and Sir Reginald's faces got redder and redder.

McDowell rushed at DeCaux, "I'll see you on a stake first
before you burn these.!" Before he could lay hands on him he was
tackled by two more knights who held him firm. They looked like they
were going to be sick from it though.

DeCaux added, "I need no confessions to burn them," he spat.
" I knew the two I had were Cathar's, so of course, all the others are
too. Maybe even some of the children."

Merena screamed at him. "Don't you dare try to harm these
children! They are all orphans that have come to us for
protection!Even you would not dare to harm these innocents!" He
shook his head, "Wrong. They are imps and sinners , spawn that will
grow up to be heretics, better they should have their souls saved now."
McDowell didn't bother struggling. against his guards, "You are one
sick bastard!" he said to DeCaux. " You hurt one woman or one child
and you will never leave here alive, will he,Brothers?" He looked
around at all of them. "Could any of you allow that to happen? Could
you live with yourself? I don't think so." The men did not move but
all of them looked uncomfortable in the silence that followed.

Just then an enclosed coach with two footmen pulled up. the
door was opened and out stepped the Bishop. "I got here as soon as I

could" he said to McDowell and Reginald standing in front of him,
"Luckily one of the nuns in Vielha slipped and told me what you
were up to," he turned to the Mother Superior.

"You go back to Vielha, and pack your things, you are not fit
to be in the same room as the lowest one in your parish." "I did the
right thing!" she screamed at all of them. The children have no
business here with these heretics, and they have no business here
either!" He looked at her sadly, "Ye without sin ,will ye throw the
first stone?" She was silent.

He looked around at all of them. There was more silence.
"Get her out of here", he told the guards by her. DeCaux was
watching everything carefully. "I am a chief inquisitor," hesaid, you
have no authority over me, I shall go on with the punishment here.I
have been tracking these heretics for months."

The Bishop's face went pale. "You are very mistaken. I know
about you. You are the one with no authority here. None. So you take
your men and get out now. The Prince of Catalonia has a special
arrangement with the pope and the king. You should know this, you
were just trying to get the job done. before you had to acknowledge
that treaty here. You should know there are many here that do not
have our faith. We must accept them according to the Prince's wishes,
and we wish to anyway. Your bullying will not be tolerated here.. "
He ran out of air and gasped. "You all should be ashamed to take his
orders. The knights Templar are not beholden to the likes of him. Go
on over to LLeida and get your new orders, learn how it's done here.
Tell

them I sent you, if they have any problem with that let them take me to task for it, but I doubt it."

He looked at Decaux who was so mad he was shaking. "As for you, if you try to arrest these people in this diocese again I will go straight to the new Pope . You may have a license to kill freely in France, but any scroll you have is not worth the ink on it here. Now all of you go quietly, and we will try to comfort these children who you have all terrified. " He looked around at all the knights with DeCaux.   " And all of you go to confession!"

All the horses were turned and men rode off. DeCaux still stood by his horse and focused his blazing eyes at the Bishop. "You will be hearing from both me and the pope very soon. You have protected a nest of heretics and two murdering knights. I do not think you will be around here much longer, and I look forward to that day." He got his horse and the Bishop said, "Perhaps neither of us will be around much longer, but I think where I'm going my odds for forgiveness will be much higher than yours."

He watched as the inquisitor rode off, and then the women and children gathered around him all talking at once. Sir Reginald went to see how the baby was doing, and Sir McDowell held tight to Merena as she broke down and cried from relief. She took his hand," David, I could not possibly leave the sisters. The have always depended on me, and now is when they need me most to get through the winter. "

He shook his head, "I need you too, look at Brother Reginald, he has devoted himself to the Temple. He wants a family, an heir, so much he is willing to adopt a child. I do not want to end up that way, I want an heir too, or two or three of them. Most of all I want you, I knew it on God's mountain." She paced in front of the huge rock, "What about the Temple? I thought knights were all celibate." He shook his head, "Oh no, not all, and we are not all warriors. Many stay in their orders for many reasons. They are administrators, manage properties, guard, run the farms. There are many different ways to serve the Temple."

"What abut the Church? I think they would frown on you living with a heretic, do you not? That is another thing, we do not do oaths. I could not make vows, could not be married in the Church, or by a priest." He was getting frustrated, " All that is workable, do you, or do you not love me? Will you or will you not marry me?" He held her to him. "Tell me, right now."

She thought aloud, " I could not leave here until Spring, there is too much I need to write down for them, I need to teach the combinations of plants ,so many other things." He picked her up , where she stood ,and sat her down on the rock, "Yes or no? If yes, I will stay with you until Spring. If no, I will leave with Sir Reginald."

CHAPTER 36

Valamos area,Val D'Aran, Catalonia, 1254 A.D.

They announced their intentions to marry the next day,

with cheers and good wishes to follow. Merena could not make an

engagement promise as it was an oath ,and Cathar's did not swear

oaths unless forced to. They had decided to ask Sister Garnier to

marry them as she had been a parfaite, a deacon, with their

religion. They also wanted Father Simon to officiate because he

had been a priest who

could perform the rites, They would each say what they wished to
from the bond between them.

Sir David asked Brother Reginald to be his best man. A note
was posted in the village store inviting those who wished to attend,
and many did as both the village and the women had reached out to
each other. to form friendships.

It was a beautiful sunny September day the wedding took
place. Sister Garnier in her new green gown and Father Simon, finally
in his is new brown monks robes had met together to share notes on
the ceremony. The baker had been busy for days creating cakes and
several of the foods for the wedding feast. Finally it was time, Merena
wore a blue velvet gown, and white veil complemented by white
violets in a bouquet. She was accompanied by the young gardener,
Sister Capelle, as Maid of Honor.

The two knights wore their polished armor and Templar capes
and swords. Most of the village turned out for the wedding and feast,
and the women were thrilled to be able to return the favor for all they
had done.

Merena simply said she would love no other, and she would
care for her husband the rest of his life. Sir David said he vowed to
make her happy, and would protect and provide for Merena, and any
family they might have. Father Simon blessed their union which is all
he felt entitled to do.

The many guests enjoyed a feast of Ptarmigan, venison, many side
dishes, fresh baked breads, spice cake, and honey walnut

cake. After the guests left Merena walked and talked with Father Simon. "I am so very happy for you", he said ,taking her arm with the free hand that didn't hold his walking stick.

"Do you know what I was thinking during your wedding?" She shook her head and stopped walking. "I was thinking of the generations I knew of your family. Not one of them was able to have a happy life with a mate except for Grandmere. Even she was cheated of a long life with her husband.

The others never even had that much. and now you have your wonderful Sir David to start a new life in Scotland, one you deserve. I am so happy I found you, and you found him. All the 'first daughters' would be happy to see it all turn out this way." She smiled,"Yes, but what about being the 'memory keeper'? How can I leave that here?" "My dear, you will just have to make new memories. ", he told her." You have until Spring, that is time to write it all down for whomever will carry it on here. You can continue wherever you go. with your first child. It will never die as long as your line survives."

The next weeks were happy ones for the newlyweds though their time together was limited as Merena gathered herbs, wrote the combinations and amounts ,for Sister Capelle who she had chosen to be her replacement. She would be the apothecary for the orphanage with others helping.

Sir McDowell was busy plowing with the basic tools the Bishop had left them, and sir Montague was chopping trees for the large amount of firewood they would need for the winter.

But that chopping became silent except for one cry of pain the very week he had planned to leave.

McDowell ran the moment he heard it happen ,and so did Merena as she planted seeds in the herb garden. They found him barely conscious under a huge , fallen oak tree. There was no getting him out. "Get Father Simon," David told her, "all his bones are broken. He needs last rites and there isn't much time, bring a quill and scroll too." She ran as fast as she could.

"Brother Montague, I am here. Help is on the way." Sir McDowell had to lean over to hear Sir Reginald, "Bury me... in Lleida -at the castle", he said weakly, "go tell the Brothers, they will get me, they then will send me back ...to England ..later...",he struggled to breathe . "Yes, I know" said McDowell, "it'll be done.".

The man went on with what breath he had left.
" Regina...stays here with Legasse. I will sign paper. She goes to... England ..then at sixteen. Legasse too..if alive. Write it all.. I must sign. My horse... for Merena."

Sir David covered the man with his cape laying there, he would not last much longer. David tried to find a place to touch him. He leaned close to talk to him, " Hold on Brother, I am with you." "You.....good friend... good man", the dying knight said,".. they will hunt her ..go home." "Rest now, they are coming. Father Simon is right here now."

Sir Reginald s looked up at him, "Need rites...going home ..". Merena

dropped to her knees. "We are here, Sir Reginald. Here is Father
Simon." The former priest wasted no time...he began his litany of last
rites as time was slipping away with his friend. "Sign..now", said Sir
Reginald. Sir David grabbed the paper and wrote what he wanted it to
say.

. "Can you sign if I hold your hand?" he said. "Sign", the
knight said. The younger knight held the paper with one hand, and the
quill in Reginald's hand. "David said, "Brother, it says all your estate
is to pass to your heir Regina Montague from here on in. You are to
be buried at the Templar castle LLeida ,and reinterred at your estate in
England, your horse to Merena, Father Simon will Witness. " The
quill was scrawled on the paper. "Yes", Sir Reginald said to someone.
"Yes..." "He is answering Father Simon's questions" ,said Mcdowell
to Merena." It's his last confession."

Father Simon continued with his prayers but Sir Reginald
was gone. David had no time to cry. "...Going to the Templar Castle in
LLeida, stay with him, don't let any animals get to him." She
nodded ,and held the still warm hand of Sir Reginald. In her other
hand she held a crudely scrawled signature that said , Baron Reginald
Montague.

She left him with Father Simon and went for torches. It would
be a long night but they would still be there in the morning when
Templar knights from Lleida came for one of their Brothers.

Chapter 37

1254 A.D. Vilamos, Val D'Aran, Catalonia

Sir McDowell had rented a small house in Vilamos for the
two of them but they went the three miles to the farm everyday, after

all there was no privacy in either open building. The work went on before the snows and ice descended from the mountaintops.

Three more children were sent from Vielha, from families with too many mouths to feed. Better to be given up as an orphan than to starve. Two girls and another boy that would pay for themselves many times over from the work they could do in the field, the kitchen, .or the schoolroom. The orphanage was now called the Montague Rescue Mission in honor of Sir Reginald Montague, who had rescued all of them. It was a mission, now,. not a convent

Whatever crops were ready had been picked, they had squash and pumpkins, they had beans and lentils, and every month had seen a small wagon load of staples sent by the Bishop until they were self sustaining.

There was already illness from the colder weather. The baby was sick for a few days but she was strong. The schoolroom was a good breeding ground for colds, but on the whole everyone was thriving in the fresh air, with a steady diet of good food.

As it got colder Merena spent more time indoors writing her potions, and balms, and poultices down. It was a long process as she jogged her mind for the number of drops, the amount of powdered root, the kinds of plants never to use or mix together. Small baskets had been woven to hold premade items to use and labeled as to the name, all kept in the gardeners room. She had already copied the long litany of the Memory Keeper for someone to take. It would have to be someone young, who had a good memory, and a love of the history that had been passed down.

She chose thirteen year old Ashtin, who had been with the women since she was five, a bright girl always interested in the old stories the women told. Ashtin would need to study the memories and learn the story of each woman they honored. There would be ample time for that as the snows came early that year, and nobody went out unless they had to do farm work.. There one one path to the stone oven and one to the latrine pit in back where the animals stayed. On those days Merena stayed with Sir David in their little house and talked , wrote her prescriptions of potions, and made their own plans.

They were happy days except for the unavoidable reminders of Sir Reginald. His horse, Starfire, now was hers.The scroll was rolled up in David's saddlebag. It had to be filed with some English magistrate on the way back to Scotland, or Scotti some still called it.

It was one of these snow -drifted days that the eldest boy came to the little house in Vilamos riding the mule. "It's Father Simon." he ran in and told them. "He's sick,Sister Garnier sent me." Merena grabbed her bag. They tied the mule and each took a horse. She rode the boy, Hunter, with her on Starfire. When they got there Father Simon was sitting in the rocking chair they had made him

. "He's been there for two days", said one of the women. "He has been sleeping sitting up because he cannot breathe." Let's get you on your pallet and prop you up," Merena said to him. "I'm alright," he said, "Just old." She said "You still need rest".

"You have been having chest pains , haven't you?" She got

him on the bed and propped him up with her own rolled up pallet she
had left there. His pained expression was all the answer she needed.
"You rest while I get you some medicine, " she told him, and dug
through her bag for the flowers she had found in June, Later, some
doctor would name in Foxglove. She showed him the purplish bell
shaped blooms that had dried into flat pieces by now." I will make you
a potion of these with honey, but I cannot give you but a little at a
time, it is of a bunch of plants called Figwort." She was back in a few
minutes with the mixture. "Let us try just a bit of this, I think you will
start feeling better, it will help your heart." He took it and the nasty
taste of the flower was eased with the honey. "Smells bad too, doesn't
it?"

He smiled. " I know my heart is giving out", he said, "you
can talk about it." She ignored him and covered him with another
blanket. "You have a chest infection, it is causing your heart to work
too hard. After we see how you do with this I will give you more
potions. I am not going anywhere, Father Simon."

McDowell sat with him and told him stories of the Temple in
England ,as she found the other prepared medicines that were kept in
the young gardener's room.. Father Simon took the knight's big hand
in his. "She does not want to let me go, " he said," but I have not long.
There is something I want you to do for me, if it is no burden. It may
be now, or it may be later, I have always thought I would like to be
buried on the little island of priest kings. I'm sure you know of it since
it is not far from Scotland. It is Iona, David, means John. The
followers

of John and Columba are buried there, John Martinus, David, some believe he was the youngest son of Mary Magdalene. He preached to the pagans there. I would be in very good company, and even though I have not met my obligations to the Church perhaps I could be buried in outlying consecrated land. Take my ashes, David, will you? And whenever you can get them there would be fine. "

Mc Dowell squeezed his hand. "It happens to be on my way home to Glen Garry, Simon, and you will be buried next to the greatest priest -warrior I can find there, for that is what you are. You must let Merena try to heal you though, we all still need you, the children need you . And it may be that you wish to return home with us in the Spring." Father Simon patted the hand holding his and closed his eyes to rest. He sighed contentedly, thinking that his friends would place him in Holy ground. Perhaps he did not deserve it but he would let the Maker decide.

Merena saw he was resting easy and so let him sleep. When he woke she gave him the same round of medicines she had given the Bishop, plus another small dose of the foxglove petals mixed with honey. They seemed to be helping his heart beat at better rate.

"I know his heart must be worn out", she told Sir David when they were in the kitchen . I am just trying to give him a while longer, a year, maybe two". Sir David held her, "You can try but he seems ready to be done with this life, after all he is almost eighty years old. He has had a good long life."

She wiped a tear off her face, "Well he the last spent ten years of it looking for me, or someone like me." Sir David wiped another tear off her cheek. "He has completed what he felt was his mission".

" My mission started with love for the Templar's, I hope it will end with me loving you ." He thought a moment. "You know, Simon has done much the same thing ,first Jongleur ,and now you. I must tell him when he wakes."

They remained there for Merena to treat him the next two days. He seemed to be somewhat better by the second night. Sir David had worked on the mountain that day cutting more firewood as the orphanage was running low and they were too cold in the schoolroom to work.

He went to the dormitory to retire early while Merena stayed with Father Simon.The monk was in a strange mood that night. He had eaten a good supper of broth and a piece of bread, even one of the baker's walnut cookies for dessert.

He seemed to want to talk , first about their time together, then about his early years at the seminary where he had studied Latin and other subjects. But what he talked about most was Jongleur, the little boy who had grown into a loving young man he never saw again. He told her more of the story left by Jongleur, and how he had lived with that story in his mind all those years. "It's what kept me going to find you", he told her, "How could I not have been as committed as he was?" he said. "You know, I have never pried into your mind, even after you told me the people and things you saw in dreams and awake, could I, this one time, ask you what you see now? For the future?"

She smiled at beloved old man, "I haven't had much time since we have been here to see much, but I will gladly tell you what I do think. Before you told me what was happening to me I just thought I was strange, now it all makes sense." She took a deep breath, "I see this farm growing into a small village with many children. I see these fields growing lots of herbs and vegetables, and several of the younger women and older children will learn how to use them to help people. I see myself with a 'first daughter' that I am naming Simonia after a wonderful man. But I will not call her that, I will call her Simi. She will have the hair color of the other 'first daughters".

The old man smiled, "Really?" he asked, she nodded and went on. " I will tell her about her Godfather and how he walked ten years to honor a request, how he watches her grow up from heaven. And Someday we will take her to this small Island where he is buried so that she may see his stone and know he was a real man."

Her eyes had a far away look. She continued, " I see a boy we will name Reginald David McDowell, with his father's curly blond hair. I see a fine lady in England who is Baroness Regina Montague. She will go from being a orphan left at the side of the road to a noblewoman, who will marry a Duke." He was still smiling, but he had one more question. "What of the Cathar's, the Bogomil's, all the other heretics? Will there be any peace for them? Will people learn to live together even though they believe different things? Will this killing stop?"

Merena looked at the old man holding her hand. "I see the next pope is a man of tolerance and love. He will bring peace to these lands," she told him. "He will be a man of change." It was a lie she felt she could live with for the good it would do, and maybe someday it might be true.

Father simon was still smiling at her, "And then you, and all the others will be safe and happy. I could even go back to the Church if I lived in that time." Father Simon, friend of Grandmere, Emmalena, Jongleur, and Merena closed his eyes and died peacefully. He had succeeded in his long mission . It was time for him to rest. He was still smiling.

Sir David and Merena did the same thing Jongleur had done for his beloved Great-grandmother Lena. They took Simon the monk to one of the fields and set his Earthly remains ablaze, then gathered his ashes into Merena's empty herb bag. He would be carried away to the beautiful Island of Iona with the two of them, come Spring.

CHAPTER 38

Toulouse, france 1255 A.D. The Villa

It has been another truly eventful month in the reports. I am told most military action has now ceased in the extermination of heretics, but the extermination itself is widely carried on by the Inquisition. The clergy has a free hand with arrest and torture, it seems. But there is less and less opportunity for mercenary soldiers to take the spoils. All goes to the Church and the King.

The Moors have been expelled in Portugal, and the missionary William of Rubriek has returned to Cyprus after failing to convert the Tarter's.

The Mongols have been sent to destroy all the Muslim states in Southwest Asia, and the Jews are now being tortured and hanged in England, most of them. The Cathar's continue to be hunted and tortured generation after generation. It is doubtful DeCaux, and others, will tire of this until they are also dead.

The old pope is dead and his successor elected is Rinaldo di Jennes, who has taken the name Alexander IV. He has already granted Sicily to Edmund, son of Henry III of England, who has failed to oust the reigning Manfred. In return, Edmund must pay the Pope 2000 ounces of gold a year, three hundred knights for three months of service, and repay the thousands of marks he borrowed from the previous pope, to war against Sicily.

This is our world today. As any future reader may see, it is a world of religious and political intolerance. I pray God it is different in your time. If it is not, perhaps this volume I have written may encourage the leaders in your time to learn from our mistakes, our intolerance, and unnecessary exterminations, whether they be for war or religion.

If you have stayed with this volume it may be of interest for you to know I have been awarded my replacement. It will take time for him to succeed me but he will be ready when he is needed, when I am gone. I was happy with the choice of the Order. He is the young shepherd from the Bugarag mountain area , a young man who has just enough loyalty to the Order to do a great job, and enough humanity to break the rules. He will be an important servant to the Order.

As for me, I am not allowed to retire,my replacement will continue to check in and assist. But if I were allowed, I think I would go to the Valley of the Valleys, Val D'Aran, in Catalonia and watch the children play in the mountain mist at the Montague Rescue Mission.. I see they now have twenty children increasing by one or two per week. It is a happy place.

I am in hopes that my replacement will continue this tome, but if not, I cannot end mine without mentioning the certain family the Order will always watch. Sir McDowell and Merena took the ashes of Father Simon to Iona as they promised . After a ceremony of honor by Scottish Templar's he was laid to rest by Knights Templar warrior-priests. He certainly earned the honor. The British Temple honored Sir Reginald Montague with a stone of service in spite of interference from Carcasonne. He was reinterred in the chapel at his estate.

As for Sir David McDowell, originally named after King David of Scotland, he manages his small estate and serves as guard to Alexander III, the young King who had knighted McDowell in his minority. The young King of Scotland is now eighteen years old, and is glad Sir David has returned to be one of his guards again..

Sir Mcdowell ,and his wife Merena have one child, a daughter they call Simi, and another child on the way. Merena may one day decide , is is said,to be an apothecary to the court after her children no longer need her.

The Order will continue to watch this family, and any other generations that spring from them, so that knowledge of all descendants shall be preserved for the future. As the Order says in many documents, 'The truth is our sacred duty, it shall not be compromised.'

THE END

Thank you for purchasing this book. If you enjoyed it please

leave a review. ' The Devil on God's Mountain', is the sequel to 'The
Chronicles of Jongleur, The Storyteller. If you have not read the epic
novel which paved the way for this volume, you may enjoy reading it
as well.

Sandra Gallimore

www.ingramcontent.com/pod-product-compliance
Lightning Source LLC
LaVergne TN
LVHW041212080426
835508LV00011B/928